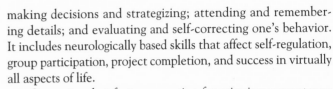

DADD Express

Volume 23, Number 4 • Winter 2012

Council for
Exceptional
Children

A publication of the DIVISION ON AUTISM AND DEVELOPMENTAL DISABILITIES, a unit of the Council for Exceptional Children

Focusing on individuals with autism, intellectual disability, and related disabilities

Teachers' Corner

Dianne Zager
Pace University

Samantha Feinman
New Frontiers in Learning

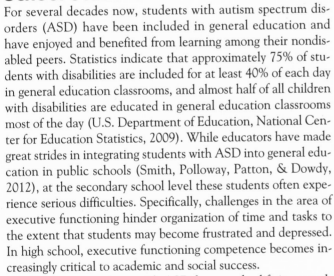

Building Executive Functioning Competence in High School Students with Autism

For several decades now, students with autism spectrum disorders (ASD) have been included in general education and have enjoyed and benefited from learning among their nondisabled peers. Statistics indicate that approximately 75% of students with disabilities are included for at least 40% of each day in general education classrooms, and almost half of all children with disabilities are educated in general education classrooms most of the day (U.S. Department of Education, National Center for Education Statistics, 2009). While educators have made great strides in integrating students with ASD into general education in public schools (Smith, Polloway, Patton, & Dowdy, 2012), at the secondary school level these students often experience serious difficulties. Specifically, challenges in the area of executive functioning hinder organization of time and tasks to the extent that students may become frustrated and depressed. In high school, executive functioning competence becomes increasingly critical to academic and social success.

To prepare students with ASD for everyday life in secondary school and beyond, today's high school special educator needs to be able to design strategies that promote independence (Kaweski, 2012). Teachers must focus on building self-determination, self-advocacy, social competence, and executive functioning competence (Roberts, 2010; Wehmeyer & Patton, 2012). These skills are necessary for independent adulthood; thus, they are part of an indispensible skill set for students with autism (Zager & Alpern, 2010).

Strategies to Promote Executive Functioning

This article provides tips for helping adolescents improve their executive functioning. *Executive functioning* relates to mental processes that connect experience to action. It is a requisite skill set for planning activities; organizing time, space, and tasks; making decisions and strategizing; attending and remembering details; and evaluating and self-correcting one's behavior. It includes neurologically based skills that affect self-regulation, group participation, project completion, and success in virtually all aspects of life.

Strategies that foster executive functioning competence include

1. providing clear expectations and directions, using concrete language;
2. providing stable environments with external structure and clear-cut rules;
3. creating time-management tools like to-do lists and intermediate benchmarks for assignments;
4. creating color-coded schedules to keep at home, at school, and in the student's school bag;
5. using organizers for desk, notebooks, and school bag;
6. establishing a daily routine with specific times for each required activity;
7. scheduling daily or weekly time to clean desk and school bag;
8. planning and scripting situations with social stories and role playing in advance;
9. teaching alternative behaviors and reinforcing adaptive behavior;
10. developing templates for common activities, such as book review forms; and
11. providing prompts that can be faded to increase likelihood of success.

Teachers can help students overcome challenges with executive functioning so that these students become better able to manage time and to prioritize and organize academic and non-academic responsibilities. For example, students may benefit from creating color-coded daily schedules that take into account different responsibilities and activities and organize these items by assigning them different colors. Classes, study time, family commitments, sports practices, music lessons, and so forth, can be assigned different colors on the schedule so that the student can visually observe the time commitment and structure of each activity and when it is occurring. Schedules should be easily accessible for students and should be utilized for ongoing reference. Students can keep copies of their schedule in a variety of places for easy access, such as their bedroom, the refrigerator, and their notebooks.

(Continued on page 2)

President's Message

Richard Gargiulo

It is hard to believe that 2012 is almost gone. It certainly has been a memorable year for many of us in so many different ways. It has been a year of tremendous pride and jubilation as seen at the Olympics and Paralympics. 2012 was also a year of despair as witnessed by the tragedy in Colorado and the onslaught of tornados and hurricanes across our country. What was 2012 like for you? Was it a good year or one you might just wish to soon forget? Would you do anything different? Did you have the chance to make a difference in the life of just one person?

It is my wish, as I conclude my term as your president, that 2013 be a year that we will all commit to making a difference. There is so much to be done and we can all play a role. I know that for many of us our time is a valuable resource; yet, I encourage each member of DADD to think about what *your* role could be. You might join a community task force concerned with bullying in our schools. You might offer your expertise to help a young adult with intellectual disability learn how to read. You may decide to actively participate in your state DADD chapter or subdivision. You may finally decide that 2013 is the year that you share an effective instructional strategy or program that benefits an individual with a developmental disability at our annual conference. No matter what you choose, the important point is that each of us does something. May 2013 be *your* year for action and involvement. Let's all commit to something that will have a positive impact on the lives of individuals with a developmental disability. No task or agenda is too small or inconsequential. Collectively, we can make a difference.

In closing, I wish to express my heartfelt gratitude and deep appreciation to an amazing group of professionals who tirelessly serve as the Board of Directors of DADD. I have known many of you for decades not only as colleagues but also as friends. Your support and encouragement has made my job of president that much easier. Thank you. As I leave the office of president, and Nikki Murdick assumes this role, it is comforting to know that so many good people will be there to offer assistance and guidance whenever needed.

(Teachers' Corner, continued from page 1)

Helping to create homework or assignment to-do lists can help students stay on top of academic responsibilities. Teachers can guide students in utilizing a daily planner or smartphone calendar to keep track of assigned homework, quizzes and tests, and papers and projects based on due dates. Each day, students can create a running tally of assignments they need to complete for the next day or next week while also crossing off tasks as they are completed. In addition, helping students break down large assignments can alleviate the anxiety and immobilization that may occur when they feel overwhelmed by a large project. Reviewing requirements of projects and breaking them down into smaller, more manageable pieces can reduce confusion and anxiety. Completing smaller tasks makes doing the work less intimidating and more manageable, and it provides immediate feedback and reinforcement for small achievements.

Conclusion

Students with ASD have been participating in general education high school classes for decades. Yet, because of these students' executive functioning challenges, teachers often struggle to instill in them organizational skills to enable them to independently complete tasks. Instructional interventions that address these difficulties have the potential to enhance academic and social performance. Teachers can help students develop executive functioning competence through strategies specifically targeted to improve organizational skills. As we prepare students with ASD for success in high school and beyond, knowledge about strategies to build executive functioning competence is essential.

References

Kaweski, W. (2012). How do we go from competent to good to great? *DADD Express, 23*(3), 1, 7.

Roberts, K. D. (2010). Topic areas to consider when planning transition from high school to postsecondary education for students with autism spectrum disorders. *Focus on Autism and Other Developmental Disabilities, 25,* 158–161.

Smith, T. E. C., Polloway, E. A., Patton, J. R., & Dowdy, C. A. (2012). *Teaching students with special needs in inclusive settings* (6th ed.). Upper Saddle River, NJ: Pearson.

U.S. Department of Education, National Center for Education Statistics. (2009). *The condition of education.* Retrieved from http://nces.ed.gov/programs/coe

Wehmeyer, M., & Patton, J. R. (2012). Transition to postsecondary education, employment, and adult living. In D. Zager, M. L. Wehmeyer, & R. L. Simpson (Eds.), *Educating students with autism spectrum disorders: Research-based principles and practices* (pp. 247–261). New York, NY: Routledge.

Zager, D., & Alpern, C. S. (2010). College-based inclusion programming for transition-age students with autism. *Focus on Autism and Other Developmental Disabilities, 25,* 151–157.

Authors' Note: The authors would like to acknowledge the support of REBA Schools, New York City, in the preparation of this article.

Meet the New DADD Board Members!

Congratulations to our recently elected board members. We were pleased to have had such an outstanding slate of nominees. The newly elected officers began their term of service to the board on January 1, 2011. We would like to encourage all members to get to know the DADD board members by joining a committee, running for an office, attending conferences, and visiting our website to obtain the latest information.

Dianne Zager, *Vice President:* Currently, Dianne is the Michael Koffler Professor in Autism and director of the Autism Specialist Graduate Program at Pace University in New York, where she founded one of the nation's first inclusive college support programs for students with autism. She has worked with students with autism and intellectual disability from the early childhood level through postsecondary education. Her DADD activities have constituted a significant portion of Dianne's professional work: she has served as the Northeast representative and chair of the Publications and Research committees. She looks forward to working on behalf of the DADD membership and the students we serve as DADD Vice President.

Dagny Fidler, *Secretary:* Dagny has been a dedicated member of CEC for more than 30 years and previously served on the DADD board in the presidential rotation. She chaired CEC's Inter-Divisional Caucus during her last few years on the DADD board. She is recently retired from Des Moines Schools and is now teaching for Morningside College and Drake University. She is president of Iowa CEC and previously served as interim secretary and co-chair of the awards committee. Dagny is looking forward to being able to serve on the DADD board as secretary and helping to move DADD forward with its goals.

L. Lynn Stansberry Brusnahan, *Midwest Representative:* Lynn is an associate professor and coordinator of autism programming at the University of St. Thomas in Minnesota and a parent of a child with autism. She is the past president of the Autism Society of Southeastern Wisconsin and served on the Autism Society of Wisconsin State Board and the Autism Society of America National Board. In her position at the University of St. Thomas she prepares teachers for the special education field. As a new member to the board, she brings a passion both as a parent and a professional to ensure growth and forward momentum for DADD.

Angi Stone-MacDonald, *Northeast Representative:* Angie is an assistant professor at the University of Massachusetts-Boston in the Early Education and Care in Inclusive Settings Program. She has worked with people with disabilities for the last 15 years as a paraprofessional, teacher, consultant, and researcher. She has been actively involved in state and local committees, organizations, and grant work with the state government to promote inclusion and adequate teacher preparation to work with children with disabilities in early childhood. Angi previously served as the DADD student governor for two years during her doctoral study and is excited to begin her work as the Northeast Representative for DADD.

Leah Wood, *Student Representative:* Leah is a first-year doctoral student at the University of North Carolina at Charlotte. She taught for six years in a self-contained classroom for students with moderate to severe intellectual disability (ID). Her graduate research focuses on raising the academic bar for students with ID, and she is interested in general curriculum access and the metacognitive strategies that will best promote the comprehension of academic content for students with ID. She considers professional involvement as tremendously important, and we are pleased to welcome her as the next DADD student representative.

A Very Special Thank You to Our Outgoing Board Members:

Teresa Taber Doughty *(outgoing Past President)*
Jordan Shurr *(outgoing Student Representative)*
Dianne Zager *(outgoing Northeast Representative; transitioning to Vice President)*
Mark Francis *(outgoing Midwest Representative)*
We appreciate your commitment to DADD!

Publication Committee Report

Michael Wehmeyer
Chairperson

New DADD Publications Now Available!

The latest addition to the DADD Prism Series, *A Guide to Teaching Students with Autism Spectrum Disorders,* edited by Darlene E. Perner and Monica E. Delano, is available from CEC (**http://www.cec.sped.org/ScriptContent/Orders/ ProductDetail.cfm?section=CEC_Store&pc=P6065**). Featuring chapters by some of the most visible leaders in the field of autism spectrum disorders (ASD), this user-friendly work for special and general education teachers is a guide to the most effective assessment and instructional strategies that promote access to the general education curriculum and meet the unique learning needs of students with ASD. DADD members can receive an **additional $5.00 discount** on the purchase of this useful resource (in addition to the discount available to members of CEC). Use the code **DADD5** when you order. This discount is available only to DADD members. Each member can purchase one book with the discounted rate. The discounted rate is in effect until June 30, 2013.

Also, don't forget the other recent DADD publications. The two-volume *Social Skills for Students with Autism Spectrum Disorders and Other Developmental Disabilities* by authors Laurence R. Sargent, Darlene E. Perner, Mark Fesgen, and Toni Cook is available for purchase through CEC. Volume 1 focuses on social skills instruction at the elementary level, complete with 50 elementary school lesson plans. Volume 2 addresses secondary education and, again, is complete with 50 secondary school lesson plans. Both volumes are user-friendly and practitioner-focused, emphasizing instruction in inclusive settings leading to social competence and social inclusion. These will be "must have" guides for instruction of social skills leading to social inclusion in school and community for the 21st century!

Does Your University Library Have the Important DADD Books and Journal?

If you are affiliated with a university, often as not you are invited to provide recommendations to your library as to those books and journals that might be of benefit to your research and teaching. It is a reality that university libraries are purchasing fewer texts and print copies of journals. If DADD publications are important to your work and to your students, won't you take a moment to request that your library subscribe to the print edition of DADD's flagship journal, *Education and Training in Autism and Developmental Disabilities* and purchase the new social skills texts and Prism? And, when you contact your library, don't forget to request the DADD-sponsored publication, *Educating Students with Autism Spectrum Disorders: Research-Based Principles and Practices,* edited by Dianne Zager, Michael Wehmeyer, and Richard Simpson. This comprehensive in scope, cross-disciplinary, and research-based work contains chapters by authors are nationally recognized for their work in the topic being addressed, almost all of whom are members of DADD. The royalties from the text are donated to DADD to further the division's mission. Ordering information can be found at the Taylor and Francis website (**http://www .taylorandfrancis.com/books/details/9780415877572**).

Call for Proposals: DADD Prism Monograph Series

The DADD Publications Committee is calling for proposals for Volume 8 in the acclaimed DADD *Prism* publication series. These short monographs, typically about 100 double-spaced pages in length, target topics of special interest to practitioners in the field of developmental disabilities. Past volumes in the *Prism* series have focused on such issues as literacy skills, differentiated instruction, and instructional strategies for students with autism spectrum disorders. For Volume 8, to be published in early 2014, proposals pertaining to topics of interest to DADD members and the field are being solicited.

All royalties generated from sales are returned to the general revenue fund of the DADD, helping to fund a variety of division functions.

A proposal should include the following information:

❏ names and contact information (phone, email, address) for each of the proposed authors;

❏ title of the proposed volume and the targeted DADD audience;

❏ 1-page overview of the proposed volume;

❏ chapter-by-chapter outline of the proposed volume, including chapter titles and a 1-paragraph summary for each chapter; and

❏ tentative timeline for the work.

For additional information, or to submit a proposal electronically, please contact DADD Publications Chair Michael Wehmeyer (**wehmeyer@ku.edu**). *Proposals are due March 15, 2013.* Each received proposal will be reviewed by the DADD Publications Committee during the April board meeting and a decision will be made at that time.

14th International Conference on Autism, Intellectual Disability, & Developmental Disabilities

Research to Practice

Council for Exceptional Children
Division on Autism & Developmental Disabilities

On behalf of the Board of Directors for CEC's Division on Autism and Developmental Disabilities, may I extend an invitation to join us in Kona, Hawaii, January 23–25, 2013, for this premier professional learning opportunity!

The 14th International Conference on Autism, Intellectual Disability, and Developmental Disabilities will integrate research and practice, reflecting the need for evidence-based strategies and interventions within this diverse field.

The program features more than 100 lecture and poster presentations. Noted speaker sessions include the following:

- ◆ Helping Children with Developmental Disabilities Learn: A New Model for Integrating Technology in 21st-Century Classrooms
- ◆ Evidence-Based Practices for Students with Intellectual Disability and ASD
- ◇ Sense and Sensibilities: An Inside View on Sensory Issues, What They Look Like, Avoiding Them, and Working Through Ones That Occur
- ◆ Good Blood, Bad Blood: Science, Nature, and the Myth of the Kallikaks
- ◆ A Model for Social Skills Instruction for Students with ASD

Conference delegates may also attend an *in-depth pre-conference training institute on ASD*, led by Dr. Brenda Smith Myles. Continuing Education Units (CEUs) will be available for conference delegates.

Our conference will be held at the beautiful **Sheraton Kona Resort & Spa** at Keauhou Bay on the big island of Hawaii.

For further information, please contact:
Cindy Perras
Conference Co-ordinator
CEC-DADD
cindy.perras@cogeco.ca
www.daddcec.org

Students' Corner

Jordan Shurr
Central Michigan University

Making Connections

A colleague of mine became Facebook friends with Sir Ken Robinson following a conversation with him at the CEC convention this past spring. Admittedly, she was the envy of our graduate student cohort for quite some time! It's funny to think how significant we can make any connection with people whom we hold in high regard, no matter how small (or real). A discussion on the trip back home from a convention can include comments such as, "So-and-so came to my poster presentation," or "I saw so-and-so eating a sandwich!" While it seems silly at times, I would like to think that this is a natural part of being a student and finding your place in the field. It is important to recognize the tremendous effect that functional life skills, self-determination, and augmentative and alternative communication—among other areas of research and practice—have had on special education and, more specifically, how they have affected the lives of individual students with autism and developmental disabilities. It is equally important to recognize that individuals—actual people—were behind these efforts; that is, individuals who at one time or another were students and were at times just trying to graduate as well. It is essential that within the field of education for students with autism and developmental disabilities, there is a continual influx of people willing to press forward, push the envelope, and sometimes to simply work hard in the best interest of these students. As students, in the early stages of entry into the field, we are in the position to study the direction and work of those who have paved the way and to recognize the connections to and similarities within our own paths. In so doing we can help to ensure a continued line of academic idols for students to come.

DADD had the opportunity to offer a drawing for student members to meet their academic idol over lunch at the previous convention. A few lucky students were able to meet and make connections with individuals within the field whom they held in high regard. Following are descriptions of their experiences.

Jillian R. Gourwitz is a graduate student at the University of Central Florida. She met with Dr. Brenda Smith Myles.

Through CEC-DADD I was able to meet Dr. Brenda Smith Myles at the CEC annual conference in Denver. Dr. Smith Myles took the time out of her busy schedule to spend over an hour speaking with me and another doctoral candidate. I am a first-year doctoral student, and having the opportunity to discuss my research ideas with an extremely knowledgeable professional was a unique, genuine experience that I will never forget. Dr. Smith Myles was gracious enough to answer my questions but also asked me about my research interests. Not only did Dr. Smith Myles inform me of additional resources that will assist me with my research, she took the time to personally send me a book on the Ziggurat Model that we discussed. Dr. Smith Myles also agreed to answer some quick interview questions for my technology course project. During our meeting we discussed issues surrounding ASD, among which

were prevalence rate increases, instructional strategies, and common core standards. I have followed Dr. Smith Myles' work since being introduced to her research during my master's program, so I was extremely excited to be offered the opportunity to get one-on-one time with one of my academic idols! I even brought a book authored by Dr. Smith Myles to get her autograph. This is an experience I am extremely grateful for and will never forget. Thank you, DADD, for setting up such a wonderful opportunity for your members!

Dawn Fraser is a graduate student at Johns Hopkins University. She met with Dr. Barbara Ludlow.

I had the unique opportunity of meeting an academic idol of mine, Dr. Barbara Ludlow, at the CEC 2012 Conference in Denver. A colleague and I had lunch with Dr. Ludlow, and it was amazing! We talked about numerous topics, including doctoral studies, dissertation topics, grant writing, and choosing the type of higher education facility to work in. She was willing to answer all of our questions and, as a true teacher, she offered helpful tips and useful advice. Dr. Ludlow described her career path and how she obtained her current position at West Virginia University. As Dr. Ludlow is also the editor of *Teaching Exceptional Children*, we were able to gain a first-hand perspective on the editing process and do's and don'ts of being a writer when submitting to a journal. This was by far the most valuable experience I had at the CEC conference this year. For those of you who are considering this opportunity in the future, here is the million-dollar answer you have been waiting for—it wasn't awkward at all! Dr. Ludlow made us feel extremely comfortable and was really interested in what we were doing as doctoral students. There was never even a split second of awkward silence! I highly recommend taking advantage of this experience to anyone who has the opportunity. Not to mention that lunch was absolutely delicious and funded through DADD, which helped with travel costs! A big thanks to Jordan Shurr, DADD Student Governor, for making this opportunity possible, and, of course, a heartfelt thanks to Dr. Ludlow for taking the time to meet with us!

Editor's Note

Ginevra Courtade

NEEDED: Great writers who are willing to share information through our Teachers' Corner and Students' Corner articles! If you are interested in sharing important information with DADD members related to strategies or ideas for teachers, please send me an idea for a Teachers' Corner article. If you would like to share information with our student constituents, please send me an idea for a Students' Corner article. One of each article is published in every *DADD Express* issue. This is a great opportunity to get your ideas out to our membership!

Please get involved with DADD! One of the best ways to start is by joining a DADD committee. Check our website for more DADD news and information (**www.daddcec.org**). If you have any questions about the newsletter, would like to contribute, or have any comments, please contact me (**g.courtade@louisville.edu**). [**Please notify CEC if you have a change of address.**] Enjoy your winter!

Executive Director Position

The Board of Directors, Division on Autism and Developmental Disabilities (DADD), announces the opening of the position of Executive Director of the division. Dr. Tom Smith, executive director since 1994, will step down from the position effective December 31, 2013. The executive director serves as the professional representative of the board and provides support to board members. The appointment is for 5 years, renewable with board recommendation; there is monthly compensation.

Specific Responsibilities Include:

- Provide support, as needed, to DADD Board of Directors
- Monitor fiscal activities of the division
- Serve as the professional representative of the board
- Maintain and update board handbook, including constitution and by-laws
- Serve as the liaison between the board and CEC headquarters
- Monitor and provide input into activities related to membership, publications, communication, subdivisions, critical issues, legislation, and fiscal management

Qualifications for Executive Director:

- Experience and record of excellence in the field of intellectual disability, autism spectrum disorders, and other developmental disabilities
- Experience at the subdivision and/or federation level of CEC
- Previous DADD board experience (preferred, but not mandatory)
- Doctoral degree (preferred, but not mandatory)
- Professional recommendations

The Board will consider applications during fall 2012 and make a selection no later than January 2013. During 2013 the executive director designee will participate in the DADD Board annual meeting at the San Antonio CEC, work with the current executive director during the year to carry out specific functions, and officially begin service as the executive director in January 2014.

Interested parties should send a letter of application, curriculum vita, and names of three references to **Dr. Richard Gargiulo,** Department of Curriculum and Instruction, University of Alabama at Birmingham, Birmingham, AL 35294 no later than October 1, 2012. Questions related to the position can be directed to Dr. Gargiulo (**gargiulo@uab.edu**).

DADD Award Nominations

The following awards are given each year through a nomination process by members and friends of DADD. Nominations will be accepted between now and February 1, 2013.

John W. Kidd Subdivision Award is given for exceptional performance by a subdivision during the past year. *Selection criteria include*:

a. Maintaining membership integrity during the previous fiscal year;
b. Engaging in innovative programming, evidenced by plans and performance presented at time of application for award; and
c. Having members actively participate in DADD activities beyond the subdivision level.

Burton Blatt Humanitarian Award is presented to an individual who reflects the ideals of the Division and has made significant contributions to the field of intellectual/developmental disabilities and/or autism. *Selection criteria include*:

a. Exceptional effort and involvement in furthering the cause of persons with intellectual disability, developmental disabilities, and/or autism; and
b. Membership in DADD.

Legislative Award is given to an individual who has demonstrated leadership in the area of legislation. Individuals are eligible for nomination if they have been involved in the development, support, and/or enactment of legislation designed to meet the needs of individuals with intellectual disability, developmental disabilities, and/or autism.

Research Award is presented annually to an individual who reflects the ideals of the Division and who has made significant contributions to the field of autism and developmental disabilities through research. *Selection criteria include*:

a. Exceptional effort exerted and involvement in furthering the cause of persons with intellectual disability, developmental disabilities, and/or autism through research; and
b. Membership in DADD.

Shriver–Kennedy Student Achievement Award is presented to a young person up to age 25 who excels in one of the following areas: academics, arts, athletics, community service, employment, extracurricular activities, independent activities, technology, and self-advocacy. Students with an intellectual disability, autism spectrum disorder, or other developmental disability are eligible for this award.

Please send letters of nomination and/or inquiries to:
Dagny Fidler, Awards Chair
dagny@mchsi.com • 515/991-2715
DEADLINE: February 1, 2013

Executive Director's Corner

Tom E. C. Smith

Hawaii, San Antonio, and Other Good Things

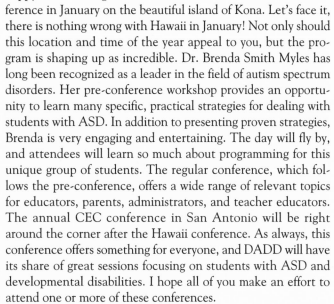

It's the time of the year to start thinking about attending CEC events. We are happy to be having our 14th DADD conference in January on the beautiful island of Kona. Let's face it, there is nothing wrong with Hawaii in January! Not only should this location and time of the year appeal to you, but the program is shaping up as incredible. Dr. Brenda Smith Myles has long been recognized as a leader in the field of autism spectrum disorders. Her pre-conference workshop provides an opportunity to learn many specific, practical strategies for dealing with students with ASD. In addition to presenting proven strategies, Brenda is very engaging and entertaining. The day will fly by, and attendees will learn so much about programming for this unique group of students. The regular conference, which follows the pre-conference, offers a wide range of relevant topics for educators, parents, administrators, and teacher educators. The annual CEC conference in San Antonio will be right around the corner after the Hawaii conference. As always, this conference offers something for everyone, and DADD will have its share of great sessions focusing on students with ASD and developmental disabilities. I hope all of you make an effort to attend one or more of these conferences.

Recently we have had a great deal of interest in starting subdivisions. If you are interested in beginning a DADD subdivision in your state, please contact me. We will provide you with a start-up kit and even include $200 in funding to get your subdivision up and running. I look forward to hearing from those of you interested in expanding our growing DADD subdivision network.

Join a DADD Committee!

Please contact the chair of any committee you may be interested in joining. See the DADD website for or information about each committee (http://daddcec.org/AboutUs/Committees.aspx)

Awards
Chair: Dagny Fidler (dagny@mchsi.com)

Communications
Chair: Emily Bouck (bouck@purdue.edu)

Conference
Co-Chairs:
Nikki Murdick (murdickn@slu.edu) and
Cindy Perras (cindy.perras@cogeco.ca)

Critical Issues
Chair: Bob Stodden (stodden@hawaii.edu)

Diversity
Chair: Elizabeth West (eawest@u.washington.edu)

Finance
Chair: Gardner Umbarger (gumbarger@woh.rr.com)

Legislative
Chair: Bob Stodden (stodden@hawaii.edu)

Membership & Unit Development
Chair: Debbie Wichmanoski (dwichman@pasco.k12.fl.us)

Nominations
Chair: Teresa Doughty (tabert@purdue.edu)

Professional Development and Professional Standards
Chair: Scott Sparks (sparks@oak.cats.ohiou.edu)

Publications
Chair: Michael Wehmeyer (wehmeyer@ku.edu)

Attention Members!

DADD members, please remember that our new website (http://daddcec.org) allows members to log in to access member-only materials (e.g., the ETADD journal). In addition, visit our site for important information about conferences and other division activities. We also encourage DADD members to **find us on Facebook** (Division on Autism and Developmental Disabilities). If members have suggestions for other materials for the website or ways we can better communicate with the members, please contact the **Communications Chair, Emily Bouck** (bouck@purdue.edu).

Volume 27   Number 4   December 2012

Focus on Autism and Other Developmental Disabilities

Contents

From the Editors
L. Juane Heflin and Paul A. Alberto   199

Bullying and Victimization Experiences of Students With Autism Spectrum Disorders in
Elementary Schools
Pei-Yu Chen and Ilene S. Schwartz   200

The Experience of Anxiety in Young Adults With Autism Spectrum Disorders
David Trembath, Carmela Germano, Graeme Johanson, and Cheryl Dissanayake   213

Using Transfer of Stimulus Control Technology to Promote Generalization and Spontaneity of Language
Trina D. Spencer and Thomas S. Higbee   225

Effect of Observing-Response Procedures on Overselectivity in Individuals With Autism Spectrum Disorders
Phil Reed, Laura Altweck, Laura Broomfield, Anna Simpson, and Lousie McHugh   237

Comparing Neuropsychological Profiles Between Girls With Asperger's Disorder and
Girls With Learning Disabilities
Megan E. McKnight and Vincent P. Culotta   247

Children With Autism: Sleep Problems and Symptom Severity
Megan E. Tudor, Charles D. Hoffman, and Dwight P. Sweeney   254

Acknowledgments   263

Los Angeles | London | New Delhi
Singapore | Washington DC

Focus on Autism and Other Developmental Disabilities (FOCUS) addresses issues concerning individuals with autism and other developmental disabilities and their families. In each issue of FOCUS, you will find practical educational and treatment suggestions for teachers, trainers, and parents of persons with autism or other pervasive developmental disabilities. Manuscripts reflect a wide range of disciplines, including education, psychology, psychiatry, medicine, physical therapy, occupational therapy, speech/language pathology, social work, and related areas. The journal's editorial staff seeks manuscripts from diverse philosophical and theoretical positions.

Types of Acceptable Manuscripts: FOCUS publishes **original research reports**; **position papers** reflecting diverse philosophical and theoretical positions; effective **intervention procedures**; **descriptions** of successful programs; and **reviews** of current books and other publications of interest. Articles cover topics throughout the lifespan in home, school, work, and community settings. Recent issues have covered employment of adults with Asperger syndrome, paraprofessionals, and augmentative and alternative communication.

Submission Guidelines: Manuscripts should be submitted via https://mc.manuscriptcentral.com/focus. At the site, under the Resources head, click on the link Instructions & Forms to obtain the journal's Editorial Policy. Authors should prepare manuscripts according to the *Publication Manual of the American Psychological Association* (6th ed.) and the journal's full editorial policy. Articles should be double spaced, using left alignment, a nonproportional font, and 12-point type. Include the title of the paper, an abstract of no more than 150 words, and 4 to 5 keywords. Figures must be provided as production-ready. Obtaining written permissions for material such as figures, tables, art, and extensive quotes taken directly—or adapted in minor ways—from another source is the author's responsibility, as is payment of any fees the copyright holder may require.

Focus on Autism and Other Developmental Disabilities (ISSN 1088-3576) (J605), an official journal of the Division on Autism and Developmental Disabilities-CEC, is published quarterly—in March, June, September, and December—by the Hammill Institute on Disabilities, 8700 Shoal Creek Blvd., Austin, TX 78757-6897 and SAGE Publications, 2455 Teller Road, Thousand Oaks, CA 91320. Send address changes to Focus on Autism and Other Developmental Disabilities, c/o SAGE Publications, 2455 Teller Road, Thousand Oaks, CA 91320.

Member Information: Division on Autism and Developmental Disabilities (DADD) member inquiries, member renewal requests, changes of address, membership subscription, and annual dues inquiries should be addressed to the CEC, 2900 Crystal Drive, Suite 1000, Arlington, VA 22202-3557; phone (toll free): 888.232.7733; fax: 703.264.9494; e-mail: service@cec.sped.org; Web site: www.daddcec.org. **Claims:** Claims for undelivered copies must be made no later than six months following month of publication. Beyond six months and at the request of the Hammill Institute on Disabilities and DADD, SAGE Publications will supply replacement issues when losses have been sustained in transit and when the reserve stock permits.

Subscription Information: All non-member subscription inquiries, orders, back issues, claims, and renewals should be addressed to SAGE Publications, 2455 Teller Road, Thousand Oaks, CA 91320; phone: 800.818.SAGE (7243) and 805.499.0721; fax: 805.375.1700; e-mail: journals@sagepub.com; Web site: www.sagepublications.com. **Subscription Price:** Institutions: $201; Individuals: $49. For all customers outside the Americas, please visit http://www.sagepub.co.uk/customerCare.nav for information. **Claims:** Claims for undelivered copies must be made no later than six months following month of publication. The publisher will supply replacement issues when losses have been sustained in transit and when the reserve stock will permit.

Abstracting and Indexing: Please visit http://focus.sagepub.com and click on the Abstracting/Indexing link on the left-hand side to view a full list of databases in which this journal is indexed.

Copyright Permission: Permission requests to photocopy or otherwise reproduce copyrighted material published in this journal should be submitted by accessing the article online on the journal's Web site at http://focus.sagepub.com and selecting the "Request Permission" link. Permission may also be requested by contacting the Copyright Clearance Center via their Web site at http://www.copyright.com, or via e-mail at info@copyright.com.

Advertising and Reprints: Current advertising rates and specifications may be obtained by contacting the advertising coordinator in the SAGE Publications Thousand Oaks office at 805.410.7772 or by sending an e-mail to advertising@sagepub.com. To order reprints, please e-mail reprint@sagepub.com. Acceptance of advertising in this journal in no way implies endorsement of the advertised product or service by SAGE, the journal's affiliated society(ies), or the journal editor(s). No endorsement is intended or implied. SAGE reserves the right to reject any advertising it deems as inappropriate for this journal.

Change of Address: Six weeks' advance notice must be given when notifying of change of address. Please send the old address label along with the new address to the SAGE office address above to ensure proper identification. Please specify name of journal.

Printed on acid-free paper

HAMMILL INSTITUTE
ON DISABILITIES

Focus on Autism and Other
Developmental Disabilities
27(4) 199
© 2012 Hammill Institute on Disabilities
Reprints and permission:
sagepub.com/journalsPermissions.nav
DOI: 10.1177/1088357612460654
http://foa.sagepub.com

$SAGE

From the Editors

We were honored nine years ago when we were asked to succeed Rich Simpson and John Kregel as coeditors for *Focus on Autism and Other Developmental Disabilities*. Rich Simpson deserves kudos for generating and germinating the idea of a practitioner-friendly journal for advocates of individuals with developmental disabilities, including autism, which adhered to criteria for quality scholarship. During our tenure as coeditors, we have been pleased to be involved with the journal in the migration to a paperless online submission and review process, inclusion as a benefit of membership in Council for Exceptional Children's (CEC) Division on Autism and Developmental Disabilities, and acceptance for indexing in *Journal Citation Reports*® (JCR), published by Thomson Reuters (formerly ISI).

As exciting as these accomplishments were, what impressed us the most during our coeditorship was the commitment and professionalism of the members of the editorial board, who not only returned thoughtful and considered comments regarding manuscripts but also were responsive to our emails querying terminology changes, policy decisions, and ideas for special issues. The unifying theme conveyed in all correspondence from board members was their passion for enhancing the quality of life for individuals with developmental disabilities, their families, and those who worked with them. We recognize that service as a peer reviewer is not only uncompensated but often occurs at the expense of avocations and personal time. We have the utmost respect and deepest gratitude for the many hours of service provided by members of the editorial board. We particularly want to acknowledge Phil Gagne, our statistical consultant, for his role in evaluating complex parametric analyses.

We also owe a debt of gratitude to our bastions at the Hammill Institute, whose guidance and support made our jobs possible as well as enjoyable. Executive director Judy Voress and publications director Peggy Kipping provided the leadership and oversight that ensured dissemination of a quality publication. Managing editor Lisa Tippett (who always seemed to be at work) spent considerable time via email and phone to lend her expertise in problem solving, production, and formatting. Administrative assistant Lee Ann Mendoza made sure that the frequently changing editorial board details were correct. Beginning in 2007, our new partners at SAGE contributed mightily to the publication of the journal. Our current production editor, Glenn Bachman, provided just the right amount of prodding and copious humor for timely publication. Finally, we would like to thank the Department of Educational Psychology and Special Education at Georgia State University for providing graduate assistants, Michelle Ivey and Carina De Fazio, who served as the glue for our efforts.

During our tenure as coeditors, we have been continually impressed by the depth and breadth of the manuscripts submitted for publication consideration. The foci of the submissions have broadened to include a greater variety of developmental disabilities, with enhanced methodological rigor leading to correlational and causal conclusions. We have moved beyond simple reporting of perceptions and attitudes to an examination of how such qualitative features affect behavior. We also have seen a shift from an almost exclusive scrutiny on young children to encompass considerations for adolescents and adults. As trends have changed, our commitment has remained that of providing meaningful implications for applied settings.

We are confident that new coeditors, Alisa Lowery and Kevin Ayers, will continue and enhance the commitment to individuals with developmental disabilities, their families, and the professionals who serve them. Dr. Lowery is an associate professor in the Human Development Center at the Louisiana State University Health Sciences Center. She has more than 10 years of experience as a classroom teacher and an equal number of years in personnel preparation. She has numerous publications related to supporting inclusion of children in educational settings and young adults in postschool environments. Dr. Lowery examines and discusses evidence-based practices and also studies applications of technology in instructional and collaborative activities. Dr. Kevin Ayers is an associate professor and board-certified behavior analyst in the Department of Communication Sciences and Special Education at the University of Georgia. After several years as a classroom teacher, he has spent the past 12 years in personnel preparation. Dr. Ayres' considerable body of research includes examination of curricula for students with severe disabilities and use of technology, particularly video technology, for promoting skills acquisition.

It has been our pleasure to work with the hundreds of authors who submitted their scholarship for review during our tenure as coeditors. We encourage the continued examination of many of the variables that affect learning and development among individuals with developmental disabilities, and the effectiveness of those who support them. We look forward to the continued excellence of *Focus* as an important masked, peer-reviewed journal, making meaningful contributions to professional literature.

Cordially,
L. Juane Heflin, PhD, BCBA-D
Paul A. Alberto, PhD
Georgia State University, Atlanta, USA

Focus on Autism and Other
Developmental Disabilities
27(4) 200–212
© 2012 Hammill Institute on Disabilities
Reprints and permission:
sagepub.com/journalsPermissions.nav
DOI: 10.1177/1088357612459556
http://foa.sagepub.com

Bullying and Victimization Experiences of Students With Autism Spectrum Disorders in Elementary Schools

Pei-Yu Chen, PhD[1] and Ilene S. Schwartz, PhD[2]

Abstract

We explored bullying and victimization experienced by third- to fifth-grade students with autism spectrum disorders (ASD), by surveying students with ASD, their parents, and their teachers. A total of 25 triads, each including one student with ASD, one of the student's parents, and one teacher, were involved in data analysis. We found that all three respondent groups reported high prevalence of bullying and victimization experienced by students with ASD. While students with ASD, their parents, and their teachers reported similar victimization scores, teachers reported significantly higher bullying scores than those found in student- and parent-reports. The three respondent groups showed some differences in bullying status of students with ASD. We discuss implications for including students with ASD in bullying prevention and schoolwide models of intervention to improve the quality of life of students with ASD.

Keywords

bullying, victimization, autism, inclusion, positive behavior support

Bullying and victimization affect students' quality of life at school and have become crucial predictors of their social, emotional, and academic development over time (Kokkinos & Panayiotou, 2004; Parault, Davis, & Pellegrini, 2007). About 30% to 40% of elementary, middle, and high school students in the United States experience bullying and victimization at school on a daily or weekly basis (Bradshaw, Sawyer, & O'Brennan, 2007; Nishina, Juvonen, & Witkow, 2005). This alarming statistic clearly demonstrates that bullying is a serious and widespread problem. Currently, there are over 2,000 published research studies about bullying and peer victimization issues from around the world. The number of studies indicates that the problems of bullying and victimization among school-age children have raised concerns and are a priority among families, schools, academia, and popular media.

Bullying and victimization are defined broadly as a socially or physically more powerful person or group intentionally attacking a less powerful person or group over time (Hunter, Boyle, & Warden, 2007; Solberg & Olweus, 2003). The forms of bullying are categorized as (a) direct bullying, including physical and verbal bullying (e.g., pushing, tripping, making fun of someone, name-calling); (b) indirect bullying (e.g., spreading rumors, threatening to withdraw friendships, ostracism); and (c) sexual harassment. Indirect bullying also can occur as "cyber-bullying" (via email, blogs, cellphone messages, and so on; Leff, Power, & Goldstein,

2004; National Center for Education Statistics [NCES], 2007). The terms *bullying* and *victimization* often have been used interchangeably in the research literature, referring to students bullying others as well as to students being bullied. In this study, we use the term *bullying* to describe students who are bullying others and the term *victimization* to describe students who are attacked in bullying incidents.

Bullies and victims are common roles that students play in a bullying situation. Students who are bullies initiate bullying and are considered to be aggressive. In addition, bullies are perceived to be stronger or more powerful than other students. This power difference can be relational or physical, such as having higher social status among peers or being physically bigger than others. Students who are victims are targets of bullying. Two types of victims are described in professional literature, including passive/submissive victims and provocative victims (Olweus, 1994). "Submissive victims often withdraw and/or cry when bullied by others and are the most common type of victim" (Swearer, Grills,

[1]National Taipei University of Education, Taipei City, Taiwan
[2]University of Washington, Seattle, USA

Corresponding Author:
Pei-Yu Chen, National Taipei University of Education, Special Education, No. 134, Sec. 2, Heping E. Rd., Da-an District, Taipei City 106, Taiwan, Republic of China
Email: pychen0337131@gmail.com

Haye, & Cary, 2004, p. 65). Provocative victims, on the other hand, tend to retaliate when victimized. The latter type of victims share personalities of bullies and victims and thus are considered as bully-victims (Swearer et al., 2004). Bully-victims who both initiate and are targets of bullying behavior are identified as a different role in the bully/victim continuum (Holt, Finkelhor, & Kantor, 2007; Karatzias, Power, & Swanson, 2002; Solberg & Olweus, 2003). Uninvolved students, including bystanders, are the fourth role that students may play in the bully/victim continuum. This type of student does not engage in bullying incidents. We wanted to examine the four potential roles students can play: bullies, bully-victims, victims, and uninvolved students. In this study, we use the term *victims* to refer to students who report only victimization experiences, whereas "bully-victims" refer to students who report both bullying and victimization experiences.

In the past two decades, researchers have investigated multiple aspects of bullying and victimization, including (a) defining bullying and victimization, (b) exploring the prevalence of bullying and victimization, (c) identifying the interactions among protective and risk factors, and (d) developing interventions to address and prevent bullying incidents in school settings. The majority of these researchers, however, have focused on typically developing school-age children. Characteristics of likely victims, as well as reports from parents of students with disabilities and adults with disabilities, suggest that students with disabilities may be at even higher risks of victimization than their typically developing peers (Dubin, 2007; Little, 2002).

Characteristics of students with autism spectrum disorders (ASD) may place them at higher risk of bullying and victimization. Students with ASD are affected by the disability in different ways, but they share the following defining features: having delays in communication and social skills, performing ritualistic behaviors, and having limited interests (American Psychiatric Association [APA], 2000; National Research Council [NRC], 2001). Depending on the number and severity of developmental areas affected, students might be diagnosed as ASD but with various labeling, such as autistic disorder, Asperger syndrome (AS), or pervasive developmental disorder–not otherwise specified (PDD-NOS; APA, 2000). Some students with ASD may have severe delays across developmental domains (i.e., cognition, psychosocial, and communication), whereas other students with ASD may have an average or above average IQ with some communication difficulties or social awkwardness. Because deficits in social interaction and communication skills are identified as common predictors of students' victimization experiences (Martin & Huebner, 2007; Storch, Krain, Kovacs, & Barlas, 2002), researchers, educators, and parents worry that these students, regardless

of the level of severity of ASD, are easy targets for bullying at school (Heinrichs & Myles, 2003; Little, 2002).

Furthermore, increasing numbers of students with disabilities, including students with ASD, participate in general education classrooms for at least part of their school day. Even students who are in segregated special education classes are most often on school grounds with typically developing students or in groups with students who may be potential bullies. According to Boyer and Mainzer (2003), in the 2001 school year, 75% of students with disabilities spent 40% or more of their school day in general education settings. Although students with special needs receive the majority of services from special education personnel, an increasing amount of academic and social needs are required to be fulfilled in general education settings by general education teachers, paraeducators, and peers. Although integrated and inclusive settings may be beneficial overall, they may expose students with ASD to more situations with the potential for bullying and victimization. Therefore, just as students with disabilities cannot be included in general education without appropriate planning and accommodation for academics, specialized supports and services also are necessary in the social domain to prevent bullying and victimization and to prepare students with ASD to respond to bullying and victimization incidents if they occur.

Several researchers have explored bullying and victimization experienced by students with ASD through parent and student surveys or interviews (Kessler, 2005; Little, 2002; Roekel, Scholte, & Didden, 2010). In two out of the three studies, however, students across the entire autism spectrum were not included. Little (2002) surveyed only the mothers of 4- to 17-year-old children with AS or nonverbal learning disorders (NLD) in 411 middle-class families in the United States. Ninety-four percent of the participating mothers reported that their children had experienced being bullied at least once in the previous year. One third of the participants stated that their children experienced indirect bullying, such as not being invited to a friend's party, being picked last for teams, and being excluded from daily school lunch groups.

Similarly, Kessler (2005) surveyed 55, 12- to 18-year-old adolescents functioning on the higher end of the autism continuum to investigate their victimization experiences at school in the United States. The majority of the adolescents (94.12%) were from middle-class families with household income exceeding US$30,000. Kessler found that adolescents with AS experienced the following direct and indirect types of bullying incidents: being laughed at (49%), having rumors spread about them (35%), clothes being torn or a personal item broken (13%), and being insulted/embarrassed by sexual talk or jokes (47%). Although these researchers described the types of victimization experienced by students with AS, the information was gathered from a single informant and focused on students' victimization experiences. In both studies, the focus was on only one type of student with ASD, those on the higher-functioning end of the spectrum, so the extent to which the results represent the victimization experienced by a range of students with ASD is not clear. In addition, the characteristics of school settings where the reported victimization experiences occurred were not explored. Hence, it is not clear whether the results represent the victimization experiences of students with ASD in inclusive or segregated school settings.

Roekel et al. (2010) surveyed 230 students with ASD who were 12 to 19 years old, their peers, and teachers to understand the prevalence of and students' perception about bullying and victimization. All the student participants were recruited from three special education schools in the Netherlands and were diagnosed with autism, AS, or PDD-NOS. No information about the socioeconomic status of the participants was reported in this study. Based on teacher and student self-report, the prevalence of bullying behavior demonstrated by students with ASD is higher than the prevalence of victimization. For example, teachers reported that 46% of students with ASD were involved in bullying more than once a month and 27% engaged in bullying more than once a week, whereas 30% of students with ASD were reported to experience victimization more than once a month and 18% of students with ASD were bullied more than once a week. Among the three respondent groups, teachers reported the highest prevalence of bullying and victimization followed by students with ASD and peers. Although Roekel et al. included multiple informants as suggested by Ladd and Kochenderfer-Ladd (2002) and Totura, Green, Karver, and Gesten (2009), the implication of this study may be limited because it was conducted in segregated special education schools.

Therefore, we sought to (a) investigate the prevalence of bullying and victimization experienced by elementary students with ASD and (b) describe the bullying status from the perspectives of students with ASD, their parents, and their teachers. Specifically, we examined whether there were significant differences among student-, parent-, and teacher-reported bullying and victimization frequency experienced by students with ASD at school. In addition, the perceived bullying roles (e.g., bullies, bully-victims, victims, and uninvolved) was compared across informants.

Method

Participants and Setting

Protection of human participants was overseen by the Institutional Review Board at the University of Washington, which approved the study. A total of 37 students, including 34 boys and 3 girls in third to fifth grade, were recruited

from 25 public elementary schools across 7 school districts in the state of Washington. The students were between 8 and 13 years old ($M = 9.6$, $SD = 1.2$) and all the students had a diagnosis of one of the conditions that comprise ASD. Nine students attended self-contained special education classes and the rest of the students were placed in general education classrooms with support from resource room services or teachers who specialized in ASD. All of the students received special education services in the same schools as their typically developing peers, and all of the student participants had access to their typically developing peers at least part of their school day. Seven students had 1 to 2 hr of access per day to typically developing peers at school, whereas the rest of the students had 4 to 8 hr of access per day to their typically developing peers. The difference in students' access to typically developing peers was based on the severity of their ASD.

According to the teacher-completed *Childhood Autism Rating Scale* (CARS; Schopler, Reichler, & Renner, 1988), 5 student participants received high CARS scores (>38), 6 students received moderate scores (between 30.5 and 37.5), and 27 students received low scores (<30). The higher the CARS scores, the more severe the autistic characteristics of the student. The special education placements and eligibility determinations documented that all students had ASD (even those with CARS scores <30), and the severity of their disabilities ranged across the autism spectrum. All but one of the student participants were verbal, and the one student who was not verbal used a computerized alternative and augmentative communication (AAC) device as his primary mode of communication. All students understood English and had the ability to either orally or physically respond to the surveys if the surveys were read aloud. Among the 37 student participants, 4 students were not able to completely finish the survey, and thus were not included in data analysis. The demographic information on students with ASD, their parents, and their teachers is described in Table 1. At the end of data collection, a total of 33 student surveys, 36 parent surveys, and 33 teacher surveys completed by 23 teachers were collected. After screening for and managing missing data, data from 25 complete triads were analyzed for the study.

Bullying Survey for ASD

Informed by several existing bullying surveys, such as the Olweus Bully/Victim Questionnaire (Olweus, 1996) and the *Self-Report Victimization Scale* (Ladd & Kochenderfer-Ladd, 2002), the authors developed the Bullying Survey for ASD, which included student-, parent-, and teacher-version surveys. The student-version Bullying Survey for ASD included a victimization scale and a bullying scale (Appendix A). The first two items on the survey asked students with ASD to report their observations of bullying

Table 1. Demographic Information on Students With ASD, Their Parents, and Teachers

Variable	n	%
Students with ASD	33	
Gender		
Male	30	91
Female	3	9
Age		
8	5	15
9	11	33
10	8	24
11	8	24
13	1	3
Parents	36	
Gender		
Male	13	36
Female	23	64
Education		
Some college	13	36
College graduate or above	23	64
Teacher	23	
Gender		
Male	2	9
Female	21	91
Teaching experience		
0–1 year	4	18
2–5 years	1	4
6–10 years	8	35
16–20 years	1	4
More than 20 years	9	39
Teaching setting		
General education	13	57
Resource room	1	4
Autism specialist	3	13
Self-contained classroom	6	26

Note. ASD = autism spectrum disorders.

and victimization incidents at school. Items 3 through 16 asked students the types of victimization they experienced, and Items 17 through 25 asked about the types of bullying the students had committed. Students with ASD were asked to respond using a 4-point Likert-type scale (i.e., 0 = *never*, 1 = *once or twice*, 2 = *three or four times*, and 3 = *five or more times*). The overall readability of the survey is at a 2.3-grade reading level. The internal consistency of the student-version Bullying Survey for ASD was $\alpha = .92$ for the victimization scale and $\alpha = .73$ for the bullying scale.

The parent-version Bullying Survey for ASD (Appendix B) was based on the student-version survey to ensure that parents provided information regarding the same constructs as their children with ASD. The parent version included 10 victimization items and 7 bullying items. Parents were asked to respond using the same 4-point Likert-type scale as in the student version of the survey. The internal consistency of the parent-version survey for this sample was $\alpha = .88$ for the victimization scale and $\alpha = .64$ for the bullying scale.

The teacher-version Bullying Survey for ASD was identical to the parent-version Bullying Survey for ASD (Appendix B). The internal consistency of the teacher-version bullying survey for this sample was $\alpha = .92$ for the victimization scale and $\alpha = .83$ for the bullying scale.

Construct Validity of the Bullying Survey for ASD

Construct validity of the three versions of victimization scale in the Bullying Survey for ASD was estimated by correlating the total scores on the victimization scales to the scores of the validated victimization scale developed by Ladd and Kochenderfer-Ladd (2002). The correlations indicated that all three versions of the victimization scale in the Bullying Survey for ASD approached acceptable convergent validity ($r = .70–.83, p < .01$). The construct validity of all three versions of the bullying scale in the Bullying Survey for ASD was estimated by a Multitrait-Multimethod approach. The correlations between the Bullying Survey for ASD bullying scale and a modified *Peer Relationship Scale* (Doll, Zucker, & Brehm, 2004) showed that the bullying scale approached acceptable convergent ($r = .51–.54, p < .01$) and divergent validity ($r = -.10$ to $.21$).

Procedure

The survey took 20 to 30 min to administer to the students with ASD and was completed in home, school, or community settings depending on parents' preferences. Before administering the survey, the first author visited with the child to build rapport and obtain the student's oral assent. Prior to administering the survey, students with ASD were asked three screening items developed by Ladd and Kochenderfer-Ladd (2002). The screening items were "Are there times when you 'have ice cream for dessert?' 'Ride the bus to school?' 'Eat breakfast at night-time?'" The scale of the screening items was modified to match the 4-point Likert-type scale used in the Bullying Survey for ASD. Students' responses to the screening items informed the first author whether the students understood the questions and could respond using the scale. All of the participants with ASD were able to respond to the screening items and were administered the survey; as mentioned, four students with ASD were unable to completely finish the survey.

The definition of bullying described by Olweus (1996), and also used by Solberg, Olweus, and Endresen (2007),

Table 2. Bullying Behaviors Described by Olweus (1996)

Characteristics of bullying	Examples of bullying behaviors
Behaviors that hurt	Say mean things to someone
Happen frequently	Make fun of someone
Done by a person or a group of people who are stronger, bigger, or more popular	Call someone mean and hurtful names
	Completely ignore someone
	Purposefully leave someone out of a group
	Hit, kick, push, or shove around
	Say he or she would hurt someone
	Say something that is not true about someone
	Send mean notes about someone

was presented orally and visually to each student with ASD. The definition described behaviors that are considered as bullying and was shown one at a time along with pictures to students with ASD. The definitions and examples are provided in Table 2.

Students with ASD listened to the questions read to them and responded orally or by directly circling their answers on the survey form. If the students with ASD had questions or seemed confused about the questions when completing the survey, the first author explained the words and provided examples to help students with ASD better comprehend the questions.

Parents and teachers who agreed to participate in the study received the survey package via mail, which included the directions needed to complete the parent- or teacher version of the Bullying Survey for ASD, a gift card for a coffee shop, and a self-addressed envelope. The adult versions of the survey took about 10 min to complete. Parents and teachers were asked to return the surveys either via mail or in person when the researcher met the student with ASD to administer the student version of the survey. Teachers with more than one student participant in their classrooms received individual surveys for each student.

Data Analysis

Descriptive statistics, including number and percentage, were reported for each bullying subgroup to understand the prevalence of bullying and victimization experienced by the elementary students with ASD who participated in the study. The four bullying subgroups (i.e., bullies, victims, bully-victims, and uninvolved students) were constructed using the criteria described by Solberg and Olweus (2003).

The same criteria were applied to describe the bullying status of students with ASD from the perspectives of students with ASD, their parents, and their teachers. The criteria for categorizing students with ASD were as follows.

Bullies. Students were considered pure "bullies" if the information on bullying and victimization scales met two criteria: (a) At least one item in the bullying scales indicated that the student bullied others at the higher two points of the 4-point responding scale (e.g., "three or four times" or "five or more times") and (b) all the items for the same student in the victimization scale were rated at the lower two points of the 4-point responding scale (e.g., "never" or "one or two times").

Victims. Students were considered as pure "victims" if they received ratings at the higher two points in at least one of the items in the victimization scale but at the lower two points in all items in the bullying scale.

Bully-victims. "Bully-victims" were the students with ASD who received ratings at the higher two points in at least one item in the bullying scale and at least one item in the victimization scale.

Uninvolved. "Uninvolved" students were rated at the lower two points of the 4-point responding scale in all items in the bullying and victimization scales.

A one-way ANOVA was conducted based on information from 25 complete triads (i.e., a student with ASD, a parent, and a teacher) for each of the three groups of informants. The same analysis was used to determine whether perceived bullies, victims, bully-victims, and uninvolved students reported significantly different victimization and bullying scores.

Results

Prevalence of Bullying and Victimization

Of the 25 triads, each including a student with ASD, one of his/her parents, and one teacher, 16 students with ASD (64%) reported engaging in bullying and/or victimization at school. Eighteen parents of students with ASD (72%) reported bullying and/or victimization experienced by their children. Seventeen teachers (68%) reported students with ASD engaged in bullying and victimization (Table 3). Overall, this finding showed that bullying and victimization occurred at high rates among these third- to fifth-grade students with ASD in public school settings. Among the three informant groups, the student self-report prevalence (64%) was the lowest, followed by teachers (68%) and parents (72%).

Perception of Bullying and Victimization

The perception of bullying and victimization was investigated by comparing the mean differences of the victimization and

Table 3. Number and Percentage of Students With ASD Identified in Each Bullying Subgroup

Scale	Bullies		Bully-victims		Victims		Uninvolved	
	n	%	n	%	n	%	n	%
Student-report	0	0	9	36	7	28	9	36
Parent-report	3	12	6	24	9	36	7	28
Teacher-report	1	4	13	52	3	12	8	32

Note. ASD = autism spectrum disorders.

Table 4. Mean Differences of Bullying and Victimization Scores Reported Across Informants

Scale	Informant	M	SD	F(2, 72)	η^2
Victimization	Student	19.68	8.38	0.415	.01
	Parent	17.92	6.96		
	Teacher	18.57	7.42		
Bullying	Student	9.2	2.76	4.13*	.10
	Parent	9.1	2.61		
	Teacher	11.72	5.02		

*$p < .05$

bullying scale scores reported by students with ASD, their parents, and their teachers. Next, the bullying status of students with ASD was investigated by describing the number of students identified in each bullying subgroup as well as examining the agreements across respondent groups regarding students' bullying status. Students' bullying status was represented by four groups: bullies, bully-victims, victims, and uninvolved students. Finally, the bullying and victimization scores of students in each bullying subgroup were compared.

Group comparison regarding overall perception of bullying and victimization. The results of one-way ANOVA (Table 4) indicated that students with ASD reported slightly higher victimization scores than their parent and teacher report, but the differences in scores were not statistically significant, $F(2, 72) = 0.415$, $p = .662$, $\eta^2 = .01$. That is, there was no significant difference among the three groups of respondents regarding the frequency of students with ASD being bullied at school. This finding showed that students with ASD, their parents, and their teachers understood the students' victimization experiences at school to a similar extent.

Unlike victimization scale scores, the results of a one-way ANOVA analysis indicated statistically significant group difference in students with ASD bullying others at school, $F(2, 72) = 4.13$, $p = .02$, $\eta^2 = .10$ (Table 3). Tukey's post hoc test analysis revealed that students with ASD ($M = 9.20$, $SD = 2.76$) reported similar bullying

experiences as their parents did ($M = 9.12$, $SD = 2.62$) but reported significantly lower incidents of bullying others than their teachers did ($M = 11.72$, $SD = 5.02$, $p = .04$). Parents' and teachers' reports about students with ASD bullying other students at school also differed significantly ($p = .04$). This finding revealed that parents had similar understanding as students with ASD regarding their bullying behaviors at school. Teachers of students with ASD, however, reported more bullying behaviors performed by students with ASD than the parent and students reported.

Group comparison regarding perceived bullying status. Although students with ASD, their parents, and their teachers did not report overall victimization scores at a statistically different level, the number of the students with ASD identified in each bullying subgroup indicated different bullying experiences reported by each respondent group. The information reported by the 25 triads resulted in similar numbers of bullies and uninvolved students but showed some discrepancies in the number of students identified as victims and bully-victims (Table 3). Compared with students with ASD, teacher-report information tended to put students with ASD in the bully-victims group ($n = 13$) more so than in the pure-victims group ($n = 3$); whereas, parents were more likely to report information that identified their children as pure-victims ($n = 9$) than as bully-victims ($n = 6$).

The mean scores of bullying scale and victimization scale, as shown in Table 5, indicated that the three respondent groups reported similar bullying and victimization scores for students in the bullies and uninvolved groups. For students in the bully-victims and victims groups, teachers reported higher victimization scores but lower bullying scores. In addition, for students in the victims group, students with ASD seemed to report higher victimization scores than their parents or teachers. These score differences reported across respondent groups, however, did not reach a statistically significant level.

We found statistically significant difference in bullying and victimization scores across bullying subgroups (Table 6). Based on student-report data, the results of one-way ANOVA indicated that the four bullying subgroups reported significantly different experiences bullying others and being bullied at school. Parent- and teacher-report data for the four bullying subgroups also showed statistically significant differences in bullying scores and victimization scores.

Because of these differences, *Tukey's Honestly Significant Difference* (HSD) tests were conducted for post hoc comparisons. Teacher-report data were excluded from the comparison because only one student with ASD was identified as a bully by teachers and thus there was no variance in the teacher-report of "bullies" to allow comparison across

Table 5. Mean Differences of Bullying and Victimization Scales Across Respondent Groups

Bullying status	Student-report		Parent-report		Teacher-report		F	p	η^2
	M	SD	M	SD	M	SD			
Bullies									
Bullying	NA		11.33	0.58	11.00	NA	.25	.67	.11
Victimization	NA		10.33	0.58	10.00	NA	.25	.67	.11
Bully-victims									
Bullying	11.78	2.89	12.50	2.43	15.08	4.80	2.18	.13	.42
Victimization	25.69	7.04	25.29	5.71	22.15	4.98	.84	.44	.84
Victims									
Bullying	8.05	1.57	7.67	0.71	8.67	1.15	.19	.83	.47
Victimization	22.45	8.51	20.22	5.14	21.33	9.24	.87	.44	.80
Uninvolved									
Bullying	7.52	0.94	7.14	0.38	7.50	1.07	.44	.65	.26
Victimization	12.26	2.61	12.00	1.15	11.38	2.26	.37	.70	.39

Table 6. Bullying Subgroups and Mean Scores of Bullying and Victimization Scales

Scale	Bullies		Bully-victims		Victims		Uninvolved		F	η^2
	M	SD	M	SD	M	SD	M	SD		
Student-report										
Bullying	NA		11.78	2.89	8.05	1.57	7.52	0.94	12.04**	.52
Victimization	NA		25.69	7.04	22.45	8.51	12.26	2.61	10.40**	.47
Parent-report										
Bullying	11.33	0.58	12.50	2.43	7.67	0.71	7.14	0.38	25.91**	.79
Victimization	10.33	0.58	25.29	5.71	20.22	5.14	12.00	1.15	14.27**	.67
Teacher-report										
Bullying	11.00	NA	15.08	4.80	8.67	1.15	7.50	1.07	7.73**	.53
Victimization	10.00	NA	22.15	4.98	21.33	9.24	11.38	2.26	9.34**	.57

$**p < .001$.

bullying subgroups. The results of post hoc analysis across student- and parent-report data showed that bullies and bully-victims reported significantly higher bullying scores than the others. In addition, bully-victims and victims reported significantly higher victimization scores than the other two groups. Among the four bullying subgroups, bully-victims reported the highest victimization and bullying scores, which indicated that bully-victims experienced more victimization than pure-victims and engaged in more bullying behaviors than pure bullies.

Discussion

We explored the bullying and victimization experienced by third- to fifth-grade students with ASD in public schools where they had access to typically developing peers on daily basis. To understand these phenomena from multiple perspectives, we surveyed students with ASD, their parents, and their teachers. Three major findings emerged.

First, all three respondent groups confirmed that students with ASD experienced bullying and victimization at high rates. Based on student-report information, the percentage that students with ASD engaged in bullying incidents was twice as much as the prevalence reported by typically developing students in the United States. Of the students with ASD involved in bullying and victimization, interestingly, no student was considered as a pure bully, nine (36%) were considered as bully-victims, and seven (28%) as victims based on their self-reported bullying and victimization experiences. Second, the victimization scores reported by students with ASD, their parents, and their teachers did not differ at a statistically significant level. Teachers, however, reported significantly higher bullying scores than students with ASD and parents. Third, the three respondent groups showed an overall high level of agreement regarding the number of students who were categorized as bullies and uninvolved students.

Concordance in Prevalence of Bullying and Victimization

The results indicated that all three groups of respondents reported a similar prevalence of bullying and victimization experienced by students with ASD—student-report: $n = 16$ (64%), teachers: $n = 17$ (68%), and parents: $n = 18$ (72%). Compared with the prevalence of bullying and victimization among typically developing students, which ranges from 30% to 40% (Bradshaw et al., 2007; Nansel et al., 2001; Solberg & Olweus, 2003), students with ASD in this study reported a higher prevalence of bullying and victimization at school. This finding confirmed that students with ASD were at higher risk of bullying and victimization than their typically developing peers (Flynt & Morton, 2004). The prevalence of bullying and victimization reported by students with ASD in this study, however, was lower than that identified for students with AS or NLD (Little, 2002) but was higher than that reported by students with ASD in schools enrolling only students with identified disabilities (Roekel et al., 2010).

The differences in the prevalence of bullying and victimization we found, as compared with previous researcher, might be due to different data collection methods, students' age ranges, and the scope of survey questions. Compared with the participants involved in the current study, Little (2002) surveyed mothers of students with AS or NLD ranging from 4 to 17 years old to understand these students' victimization experiences across home and school settings and the results revealed a high prevalence of victimization (94%). According to Holt, Kaufman-Kantor, and Finkelhor (2009), parents tended to consider their children as victims and underestimated their children's bullying behaviors; therefore, the high prevalence reported by Little was understandable. In addition, the prevalence of victimization experiences examined by Little included home and school and thus was expected to be higher than rates found in only school settings. Finally, the mother-report information reflected victimization experiences from a wide age range of students. As students in middle school reported more peer victimization than students in elementary or high schools (Nansel et al., 2001), the age range of students with AS or NLD also might increase the overall prevalence of victimization identified by Little. Given the differences in data collection method and age range of students, it was understandable that the prevalence of bullying and victimization reported by Little was higher than the prevalence reported in this study.

Roekel et al. (2010) investigated the prevalence of bullying and victimization by surveying 12- to 19-year-old students with ASD, their peers, and teachers in segregated special education schools. Compared with the current study, the teacher- and student-report prevalence of bullying and victimization were lower than the prevalence identified in this study. The differences in the prevalence might be a result of the setting where the study was conducted. According to Roekel et al., the low social competence of students with ASD might be less exceptional in a school serving only children with disabilities and thus reduced the victimization rate experienced by students with ASD. As about two thirds of the student participants in this study had 4 to 8 hr of access to their typically developing peers, their characteristics of ASD, such as low social competence, might make these students stand out and put them at higher risk for bullying and victimization than the students in the Roekel et al. study. Although the prevalence of bullying and victimization identified in this study differed from the findings of previous studies, the finding of this study was considered valid given the scope of the survey questions and the relative consistent report across students with ASD, their parents, and their teachers.

Bullying Status

Compared with parent-report information, the information reported by teachers categorized more students with ASD as bully-victims, whereas parent-report information put more students with ASD in the victims group. Overall, student- and teacher-reported information resulted in similar patterns of bullying status of students with ASD, whereas teacher- and parent-reported information showed relatively low concordance especially in the bully-victims and victims groups. In addition to parents' attitudes toward their children's bullying status as mentioned in the previous section, these findings also were consistent with those reported by Totura et al. (2009), who claimed that teachers tended to report more bullies or bully-victims. The discrepancy of the information collected across respondent groups also might be derived from their sources of information (Ladd & Kochenderfer-Ladd, 2002). That is, respondents who did not share a common context, such as parents and teachers, would show lower concordance of their reports.

The information reported across the three respondent groups, however, did put about one third of students with ASD in the uninvolved students group and very few students with ASD in the pure-bullies group. The common characteristics shared by students with ASD, such as being unaware of social reciprocity and the intention of others, might help explain the percentage of students in the uninvolved group. That is, some students with ASD might not be aware of the behaviors of their peers or might not be responsive to interaction (NRC, 2001), and thus were not involved in bullying incidents. The low number of students categorized in the pure-bullies group might be related to the communication deficits and social cognitive impairments shared by students of ASD. Some students with ASD might communicate through inappropriate behaviors, such as aggression (NRC, 2001). As the intention was to communicate but not to hurt someone, these behaviors of students with ASD might not be considered as bullying by the three respondent groups.

Another shared characteristic of ASD, impairments in developing theory of mind, might affect students' ability to understand the intention of their peers' behavior (Baron-Cohen, Jolliffe, Mortimore, & Robertson, 1997). Because more than half of the student participants in this study received low CARS scores, these students with ASD might be aware of their social environment but misread the intention of others' behaviors (Happé, 1995; Steele, Joseph, & Tager-Flusberg, 2003). Furthermore, according to Carothers and Taylor (2004), high-functioning students with ASD and students with AS tend to choose aggressive strategies in social conflict situations. As a result, students with ASD in this study might perform aggressive behaviors based on their misinterpretation of the intention of their peers' behaviors and thus were categorized more as bully-victims but not pure bullies by the three respondent groups.

Perception About Being Bullied

The results of ANOVA were used to conclude that although students with ASD reported slightly higher victimization mean scores than their parents and their teachers, the differences among the three respondent groups did not differ from each other at a statistically significant level. That is, students with ASD, their parents, and their teachers showed similar understanding about the frequency of the students being bullied at school. This finding, however, was not consistent with previous literature. According to Bradshaw et al. (2007), elementary school staff tend to underestimate typically developing students' bullying and victimization experiences. Similarly, Fekkes, Pijpers, and Verloove-Vanhorick (2005) surveyed typically developing students between ages of 9 and 11 years and the results showed that about 39% and 35%, respectively, of the students thought parents and teachers were not aware of their bullying and victimization experiences at school. The lack of differences in victimization experiences reported by students with ASD, their parents, and their teachers in this study could be related to a number of variables.

First, as described in the previous section, the majority of students with ASD had impairments in developing theory of mind (Baron-Cohen et al., 1997), such as telling a

joke from a lie and understanding intention (Steele et al., 2003). Compared with typically developing peers, Carothers and Taylor (2004) found that students with ASD tended to consider a peer as "not mean" when shown ambiguous social cues. The difficulties in interpreting social cues and intention might underestimate the real victimization incidents experienced by students with ASD at school settings. In addition, the differences among the respondent groups might be influenced by the frequency of communication that parents had with their children and their children's teachers. According to Matsunaga (2009), more regular and routine family interaction was associated with less discrepancy of awareness of victimization reported by parent and children dyads. Parent participants in this study reported communicating between once a week and a few times a week with their children and their children's teachers. As a result of frequent communication, both parents and teachers would be more aware of students' school life. Finally, the findings of this study were based on a small sample and thus did not yield sufficient statistical power to capture small differences of the victimization experiences reported across respondent groups. In other words, had the sample size been larger, the differences between groups might have been statistically significant. Therefore, it was understandable that parents and teachers in this study reported similar prevalence and victimization scores as students with ASD.

Perception About Bullying Others

Group differences regarding bullying behaviors reported across respondents were consistent with the research hypothesis and previous literature. That is, teachers reported more bullying behaviors performed by students with ASD than students with ASD and their parents did at a statistically significant level. Similar findings were identified among teachers and typically developing students in kindergarten, first, fifth, and seventh grades (Monks, Smith, & Swettenham, 2003; Peets & Kikas, 2006). No statistical difference, however, was identified between parent- and student-reported frequencies of bullying behaviors in this study, which might be confounded by the data collection methods used.

In this study, students with ASD were individually surveyed about their bullying and victimization experiences. During the survey process, students with milder ASD, who comprised more than 60% of the student participants, might not have felt comfortable reporting their bullying behaviors to either their parents or the researchers due to ethical concerns or fear of encountering negative consequences (Peets & Kikas, 2006; Salmivalli & Isaacs, 2005). Students with more severe ASD, however, might not have understood the definition of bullying or have been unaware of their own behaviors and thus reported fewer bullying behaviors. As most of the parents obtained information about bullying and victimization from their children, it was understandable that parents would underestimate their children's bullying behaviors at school.

Implication for Intervention and Future Research

We extended previous literature with this study by investigating the bullying and victimization phenomenon experienced by elementary students with ASD, and the interpretation of the current findings shed future implications of including students with ASD in schoolwide behavioral support models. In the past 15 years, the paradigm of bullying intervention, as well as special education interventions, has shifted from focusing on individual students to providing schoolwide support. In addition, this shift has moved from reactive solutions to more proactive prevention. As a result, intervention programs have moved beyond individual and classroom levels to multitiered prevention programs, including schoolwide, small group, and individual-level interventions. Intervention models have been proposed to prevent students' behavioral and academic problems (e.g., schoolwide positive behavior support and Response to Intervention) as well as bullying incidents at school (e.g., the Olweus Bullying Prevention Program). These multitiered programs set up the stage for successfully including students with ASD in interventions by having consistent expectations and providing multiple practice opportunities across areas in school settings. In addition, the individual-level intervention built into these multitiered prevention programs could directly address the needs of students with ASD, such as teaching emotion recognition. Although the concepts of multitiered interventions support inclusive education for all students, students with disabilities, including students with ASD, were usually not included in schoolwide and group-level interventions.

Based on the results of this study, we can conclude that students with ASD were part of the bullying and victimization problem. Students with ASD who reported bullying and victimization experiences (64%) were potential teaching targets for bullying intervention and schoolwide approaches to promote their quality of life at school. Our data also highlight that not all students with ASD were victims. Many of these students were bully-victims and might need different interventions than pure-victims. As this study was based on elementary school-aged students with ASD, their parents, and their teachers, future researchers might include older students or adults with ASD to help identify

key skills and strategies to deal with bullying and victimization at school.

For students who engage in chronic bullying or victimization, Bowen, Ashcraft, Jenson, and Rhode (2008) and Ross, Horner, and Stiller (2010) proposed incorporating the processes of Functional Behavior Assessment and Behavior Intervention Plan as individual-level interventions to address bullying and victimization behaviors. Bowen et al. further described interventions strategies for chronic victims, such as increasing adult support through frequent check-ins, using a peer buddy system, teaching social skills, and involving parents. For chronic bullies, Bowen at al. proposed to incorporate a check-in/check-out system and strategies used in applied behavior analysis, such as self-management through behavior contract, overcorrection, and time-out. Although these interventions for bullies were not developed specifically for students with ASD, the effects of strategies are supported by previous literature in managing challenging behaviors of students with ASD (Alberto & Troutman, 2009).

Future researchers need to consider how to appropriately include children with ASD and other disabilities in schoolwide prevention and support programs. This means that we may need to investigate how to modify the content of programs so that all students (e.g., those who are nonverbal, English language learner (ELL), or have cognitive deficits) can access the content being taught. We also need to investigate if issues around disabilities and other types of difference need to be taught explicitly to all students. As researchers interested in schoolwide approaches, as well as students with disabilities, it is incumbent on us to insure that schoolwide intervention programs include and are effective for all students.

Conclusion

We conducted our study as a preliminary attempt to help educators and researchers understand the prevalence of bullying and victimization experienced by elementary-aged students with ASD. The findings of this study can be used to conclude that bullying and victimization occur among elementary students with ASD at high rates. Students with ASD, their parents, and their teachers showed high agreement regarding the prevalence of bullying and victimization experienced by students with ASD but had different perceptions about students' overall bullying behaviors. Although the limitation of the small sample size and design influenced the interpretation and generalization of the findings of this study, the information provided by students with ASD, their parents, and their teachers still shed lights for future bullying and victimization intervention and research for students with ASD.

Appendix A

Bullying Survey for ASD: Student Version

I will think about what has happened in this school year to answer these questions.

	Never	Once or twice	Three or four times	Five or more times
1. I saw students being mean to other students in school.	0	1	2	3
2. Students in my class were mean to other students.	0	1	2	3
3. One or more students said mean things to me.	0	1	2	3
4. One or more students made fun of me.	0	1	2	3
5. One or more students called me names.	0	1	2	3
6. One or more students said he/she would hurt me.	0	1	2	3
7. One or more students broke or took my things.	0	1	2	3
8. One or more students picked on me at school.	0	1	2	3
9. One or more students hit or kicked me.	0	1	2	3
10. One or more students hurt my feelings.	0	1	2	3
11. One or more students left me out of a group on purpose in class.	0	1	2	3
12. One or more students left me out of a group on purpose during lunch.	0	1	2	3
13. One or more students left me out of a group on purpose on the playground.	0	1	2	3
14. One or more students said bad things about me to other kids.	0	1	2	3
15. One or more students told a lie about me.	0	1	2	3
16. I did not want to go to school because I was worried students would hurt me.	0	1	2	3
17. I made fun of other students.	0	1	2	3
18. I called other students names.	0	1	2	3
19. I said I would hurt other students.	0	1	2	3
20. I broke or hid other student's things.	0	1	2	3
21. I hurt other students with my hands, feet, or mouth (like kicking or hitting).	0	1	2	3
22. I did not let other students join my group in class.	0	1	2	3
23. I did not let other students join my group during lunch.	0	1	2	3
24. I did not let other students join my group on the playground.	0	1	2	3
25. I told a lie about other students.	0	1	2	3

Appendix B

Bullying Survey for ASD: Parent and Teacher Version

	Never	Once or twice	Three or four times	Five or more times
In this school year, my child/this student has *experienced* the following:				
(1) being picked on by other children	0	1	2	3
(2) being excluded from groups	0	1	2	3
(3) being laughed at	0	1	2	3
(4) being hit or kicked by other children	0	1	2	3
(5) being threatened with physical harm	0	1	2	3
(6) being teased or made fun of by peers	0	1	2	3
(7) being called names by peers	0	1	2	3
(8) having peers who say negative things about him or her to other children	0	1	2	3
(9) having personal property destroyed/stolen/hidden	0	1	2	3
(10) having rumors spread about him/her	0	1	2	3

(continued)

Appendix B (continued)

	Never	Once or twice	Three or four times	Five or more times
In this school year, my child/this student has *done* the following:				
(1) excluding someone from his/her group	0	1	2	3
(2) laughing at someone	0	1	2	3
(3) threatening to physically hurt someone	0	1	2	3
(4) calling someone else names	0	1	2	3
(5) attacking someone physically	0	1	2	3
(6) destroying/ stealing/hiding others students' stuff	0	1	2	3
(7) spreading rumors about other children	0	1	2	3
(8) In this school year, my child/this student has refused to go to school because he/she was worried about being bullied at school.	0	1	2	3

Declaration of Conflicting Interests

The author(s) declared no potential conflicts of interest with respect to the research, authorship, and/or publication of this article.

Funding

The author(s) received no financial support for the research, authorship, and/or publication of this article.

References

Alberto, P., & Troutman, A. (2009). *Applied behavior analysis for teachers*. Columbus, OH: Merrill.

American Psychiatric Association. (2000). *Diagnostic and statistical manual of mental disorders* (4th ed., text rev.). Washington, DC: Author.

Baron-Cohen, S., Jolliffe, T., Mortimore, C., & Robertson, M. (1997). Another advanced test of theory of mind: Evidence from very high functioning adults with autism or Asperger Syndrome. *Journal of Child Psychology and Psychiatry, 38*, 813–822.

Bowen, J., Ashcraft, P., Jenson, W. R., & Rhode, G. (2008). *The tough kid bully blockers book: 15-minute lessons for preventing and reducing bullying*. Eugene, OR: Pacific Northwest.

Boyer, L., & Mainzer, R. W. (2003). Who's teaching students with disabilities? A profile of characteristics, licensure status, and feelings of preparedness. *Teaching Exceptional Children, 35*, 8–11.

Bradshaw, C. P., Sawyer, A. L., & O'Brennan, L. M. (2007). Bullying and peer victimization at school: Perceptual differences between students and school staff. *School Psychology Review, 36*, 361–382.

Carothers, D. E., & Taylor, R. L. (2004). Social cognitive processing in elementary school children with Asperger syndrome. *Education and Training in Developmental Disabilities, 39*, 177–187.

Doll, B., Zucker, S., & Brehm, K. (2004). *Resilient classrooms: Creating healthy environments for learning*. New York, NY: Guilford.

Dubin, N. (2007). *Asperger syndrome and bullying: Strategies and solutions*. London, England: Jessica Kinsley.

Fekkes, M., Pijpers, F. I. M., & Verloove-Vanhorick, S. P. (2005). Bullying: Who does what, when and where? Involvement of children, teachers and parents in bullying behavior. *Health Education Research Theory and Practice, 20*, 81–91.

Flynt, S. W., & Morton, R. C. (2004). Bullying and children with disabilities. *Journal of Instructional Psychology, 31*, 330–333.

Happé, F. G. E. (1995). The role of age and verbal ability in the theory of mind task performance of subjects with autism. *Child Development, 66*, 843–855.

Heinrichs, R., & Myles, B. S. (2003). *Perfect targets: Asperger syndrome and bullying: Practical solutions for surviving the social world*. Shawnee Mission, KS: AAPC.

Holt, M. K., Finkelhor, D., & Kantor, K. G. (2007). Hidden forms of victimization in elementary students involved in bullying. *School Psychology Review, 36*, 345–360.

Holt, M. K., Kaufman-Kantor, G., & Finkelhor, D. (2009). Parent/child concordance about bullying involvement and family characteristics related to bullying and peer victimization. *Journal of School Violence, 8*, 42–63.

Hunter, S. C., Boyle, J. M., & Warden, D. (2007). Perceptions and correlates of peer-victimization and bullying. *British Journal of Education Psychology, 77*, 797–810.

Karatzias, A., Power, K. G., & Swanson, V. (2002). Bullying and victimization in Scottish secondary schools: Same or separate entities? *Aggressive Behavior, 28*, 45–61.

Kessler, E. (2005). *A comparative study of sensory profiles and the perceptions of bullying with adolescents with Asperger syndrome* (Unpublished doctoral dissertation). University of Kansas, Lawrence.

Kokkinos, C. M., & Panayiotou, G. (2004). Predicting bullying and victimization among early adolescents: Associations with disruptive behavior disorders. *Aggressive Behavior, 30*, 520–533.

Ladd, G., & Kochenderfer-Ladd, B. (2002). Identifying victims of peer aggression from early to middle childhood: Analysis of cross-informant data for concordance, estimation of relational adjustment, prevalence of victimization, and characteristics of identified victims. *Psychological Assessment, 14,* 74–96.

Leff, S. S., Power, T. J., & Goldstein, A. B. (2004). Outcome measures to assess the effectiveness of bullying-prevention programs in the schools. In D. L. Espelage & S. M. Swearer (Eds.), *Bullying in American schools: A social-ecological perspective on prevention and intervention* (pp. 269–294). Mahwah, NJ: Lawrence Erlbaum.

Little, L. (2002). Middle-class mothers' perceptions of peer and sibling victimization among children with Asperger's syndrome and nonverbal learning disorders. *Issues in Comprehensive Pediatric Nursing, 25,* 43–57.

Martin, K. M., & Huebner, E. S. (2007). Peer victimization and prosocial experiences and emotional well-being of middle school students. *Psychology in the Schools, 44,* 199–208.

Matsunaga, M. (2009). Parents don't (always) know their children have been bullied: Parent-child discrepancy on bullying and family-level profile of communication standards. *Human Communication Research, 35,* 221–248.

Monks, C. P., Smith, P. K., & Swettenham, J. (2003). Aggressors, victims and defenders in preschool: Peer, self and teacher reports. *Merrill-Palmer Quarterly, 49,* 453–469.

Nansel, T. R., Overpeck, M., Pilla, R. S., Ruan, W. J., Simons-Morton, B., & Scheidt, P. (2001). Bullying behaviors among US youth: Prevalence and association with psychosocial adjustment. *Journal of the American Medical Association, 285,* 2094–2100.

National Center for Education Statistics. (2007). *School crime supplement to the national crime victimization survey (SCS/NCVS).* Retrieved from http://nces.ed.gov/programs/crime/surveys.asp

National Research Council. (2001). *Educating children with autism.* Washington, DC: National Academy Press.

Nishina, A., Juvonen, J., & Witkow, M. R. (2005). Sticks and stones may break my bones, but names will make me feel sick: The psychosocial, somatic, and scholastic consequences of peer harassment. *Journal of Clinical Child & Adolescent Psychology, 34,* 37–48.

Olweus, D. (1994). Annotation: Bullying at school: Basic facts and effects of a school-based intervention program. *Journal of Child Psychology and Psychiatry, 35,* 1171–1190.

Olweus, D. (1996). *The Revised Olweus Bully/Victim Questionnaire. Mimeo, Research Center for Health Promotion (HEMIL).* Bergen, Norway: University of Bergen.

Parault, S. J., Davis, H. A., & Pellegrini, A. D. (2007). The social contexts of bullying and victimization. *Journal of Early Adolescence, 27,* 145–174.

Peets, K., & Kikas, E. (2006). Aggressive strategies and victimization during adolescence: Grade and gender differences, and cross-informant agreement. *Aggressive Behavior, 32,* 48–79.

Roekel, E. V., Scholte, R. H., & Didden, R. (2010). Bullying among adolescents with autism spectrum disorders: Prevalence and perception. *Journal of Autism and Developmental Disorders, 40,* 63–73.

Ross, S., Horner, R., & Stiller, B. (2010). *Bullying prevention manual (elementary level).* Retrieved from http://www.pbis.org/pbis_resource_detail_page.aspx?PBIS_ResourceID=785

Salmivalli, C., & Isaacs, J. (2005). Prospective relations among victimization, rejection, friendlessness, and children's self- and peer-perceptions. *Child Development, 76,* 1161–1171.

Schopler, E., Reichler, R. J., & Renner, B. R. (1988). *The Childhood Autism Rating Scale (CARS) for diagnostic screening and classification of autism.* Los Angeles, CA: Western Psychological Services.

Solberg, M. E., & Olweus, D. (2003). Prevalence estimation of school bullying with the Olweus Bully/Victim Questionnaire. *Aggressive Behavior, 29,* 239–268.

Solberg, M. E., Olweus, D., & Endresen, I. M. (2007). Bullies and victims at school: Are they the same pupils? *British Journal of Educational Psychology, 77,* 441–464.

Steele, S., Joseph, R. M., & Tager-Flusberg, H. (2003). Brief report: Developmental change in theory of mind abilities in children with Autism. *Journal of Autism and Developmental Disorders, 33,* 461–467.

Storch, E. A., Krain, A. L., Kovacs, A. H., & Barlas, M. E. (2002). The relationship of communication beliefs and abilities to peer victimization in elementary school children. *Child Study Journal, 32,* 231–239.

Swearer, S. M., Grills, A. E., Haye, K. M., & Cary, P. T. (2004). Internalizing problems in students involved in bullying and victimization: Implications for intervention. In D. L. Espelage & S. M. Swearer (Eds.), *Bullying in American schools: A social-ecological perspective on prevention and intervention* (pp. 63–83). Mahwah, NJ: Lawrence Erlbaum.

Totura, C. M., Green, A., Karver, M. S., & Gesten, E. L. (2009). Multiple informants in the assessment of psychological, behavioral, and academic correlates of bullying and victimization in middle school. *Journal of Adolescence, 32,* 193–211.

HAMMILL INSTITUTE
ON DISABILITIES

Focus on Autism and Other
Developmental Disabilities
27(4) 213–224
© 2012 Hammill Institute on Disabilities
Reprints and permission:
sagepub.com/journalsPermissions.nav
DOI: 10.1177/1088357612454916
http://foa.sagepub.com
SAGE

The Experience of Anxiety in Young Adults With Autism Spectrum Disorders

David Trembath, PhD[1], Carmela Germano, MBSc[1],
Graeme Johanson, PhD[2], and Cheryl Dissanayake, PhD[1]

Abstract

Anxiety is known to be common among young adults with autism spectrum disorders (ASD), yet little is known about the nature of their experiences or the strategies they use to live and cope with their reported anxiety. In this qualitative study, we began to address this issue through two focus groups involving 11 young adults with ASD, and 10 parents and professionals. Participants in each group were asked to discuss the triggers for anxiety, the consequences of anxiety, and strategies they have used, would like to use, or have seen individuals with ASD use to manage their anxiety. The participants identified multiple personal and environmental sources of anxiety, noting the substantial impact they have on their everyday lives at home, work, university, and in the community. Their individual experiences and strategies for living and coping with anxiety are presented.

Keywords

autism spectrum disorders, anxiety, qualitative, coping

Anxiety is common among people with autism spectrum disorders (ASD; Bellini, 2004; Drahota, 2009; Kim, Szatmari, Bryson, Streiner, & Wilson, 2000). Individuals with ASD experience a variety of symptoms of anxiety, including physiological arousal and panic (Bellini, 2006), which can greatly interfere with their daily lives. Individuals with ASD also are reported to have poor stress management skills (White, Oswald, Ollendick, & Scahill, 2009). Understanding the phenomenology of anxiety in this population from their own perspective has immense clinical value and would be useful in devising suitable intervention strategies to minimize the adverse experience of symptoms (Gillott & Standen, 2007).

ASD is an umbrella term used to describe a group of lifelong pervasive developmental disorders, which include autistic disorder, Asperger's disorder, and pervasive developmental disorder–not otherwise specified (PDD-NOS). Each is characterized by impairments in social interaction, communication, and restricted and repetitive behaviors and interests (American Psychiatric Association, 2000). Because many people with ASD have an associated intellectual disability (ID), those individuals without a comorbid ID are referred to as having "high-functioning" autism (HFA). They function within the average or above average range of intellectual ability. Although anxiety is commonly experienced by individuals with ASD, it appears to be more prevalent among individuals with HFA, especially during transition between childhood and adolescence (White et al., 2010).

To gain a deeper understanding of the everyday experiences of anxiety in young adults with ASD, we report the outcomes from two focus groups. Our aim was to examine first-person accounts to allow those individuals affected to speak for themselves, using their own words, to explain the impact of anxiety on their lives at home, school, and community. To date, researchers studying anxiety in ASD have focused on comparing the prevalence of anxiety in individuals with ASD with typically developing controls, through the use of standardized measures and questionnaires. It is important to note that in this study, participants were asked to speak about anxiety in terms of what they understood the term to mean, with the view to generating information to inform future researchers and the development of practical strategies. Thus, our aim was not to examine the extent to which symptoms described by participants may fit within the clinical range but rather to explore the impact of self-reported anxiety on everyday life.

[1]La Trobe University, Melbourne, Victoria, Australia
[2]Monash University, Melbourne, Victoria, Australia

Corresponding Author:
Cheryl Dissanayake, PhD, Olga Tennison Autism Research Centre, School of Psychological Science, La Trobe University, Melbourne, Victoria 3086, Australia
Email: c.dissanayake@latrobe.edu.au

The Nature of Anxiety

When examining the nature of anxiety, it is pertinent to explore the factors that lead or contribute to feelings of anxiety (the *triggers*—sources of or situations that elicit anxiety), the emotional or behavioral responses that result from these feeling (the *consequences*—what happens when anxiety has been triggered), and the potential approaches that alleviate the feelings of anxiety (the *solutions*—what anxiety-reducing strategies work for individuals with ASD). An examination of the triggers and consequences of anxiety is of great practical value because proposed solutions should alleviate anxiety experienced by individuals with ASD in everyday life (Gillott, Furniss, & Walter, 2001).

Triggers

It has been well documented that a range of personal factors (e.g., temperament, behavioral inhibition), family factors (e.g., parent–child attachment, marital conflict), and environmental factors (e.g., death in family, change in marital status) can lead to the development of anxiety in the general population (Grover, Ginsburg, & Ialongo, 2005). However, there is evidence that the inherent difficulties in social awareness and social understanding experienced by individuals with ASD may act as additional triggers for anxiety (White et al., 2010). For example, Bellini (2006) examined the relationships among social skills, physiological arousal, and social anxiety in a group of 41 young people, ages 12 to 18 years, with autistic disorder ($n = 19$), Asperger's disorder ($n = 16$), and PDD-NOS ($n = 6$). Based on self-report measures, including *the Social Skills Rating System* (Gresham & Elliot, 1990), the *Social Anxiety Scale for Adolesc*ents (La Greca, 1999), and the *Multidimensional Anxiety Scale for Children* (March, 1999), Bellini reported that heightened physiological arousal and social skills deficits may contribute to social anxiety in individuals with ASD. Evans, Canavera, Kleinpeter, Maccubbin, and Taga (2005) administered a parent-report fear survey composed of 69 items rated along a 5-point Likert-type scale for 23 children with ASD ($M = 9.20$ years). Analyzed with comparison groups of typically developing children and children with Down syndrome who were matched on mental age, the children with ASD exhibited more social anxiety and had fears of specific environments and situations, such as confined spaces and medical situations.

Gillott et al. (2001) identified environmental triggers of anxiety in young people with ASD in their study of anxiety and social worry in 15 children with HFA (ages 8–12 years), and two age- and gender-matched comparison groups (15 typically developing children and 15 children with a specific language impairment). Based on the results of the *Spence Children's Anxiety Scale* (Spence, 1997) and the *Spence Social Worries Questionnaire* (Spence, 1995), the authors found that children with HFA were more anxious than children in the two comparison groups, experiencing social worries that included difficulties predicting others' behavior and readily determining what will happen next. These worries were exacerbated by unanticipated changes in the environment or in the sequence of events. This finding is consistent with previous reports that even minor changes in the environment may elicit stress, confusion, and anxiety in individuals with ASD. Indeed, the fear of possible change can be overwhelming due to the need to preserve sameness (Gillott et al., 2001).

Consequences

Gillott et al. (2001) highlighted not only triggers for anxiety in young people with ASD but also many consequences. The 15 participants with HFA (ages 8–12 years) reportedly ruminated over their worries and actively avoided social interaction with others. The authors noted that anxiety-provoking situations may result in adaptive and maladaptive behaviors used as self-calming strategies. Bellini (2004) identified a range of consequences associated with anxiety for 41 adolescents ages 12 to 18 years ($M = 14.22$ years) with ASD. These included physiological manifestations such as arousal, sensory sensitivities, panic attacks, agitation, and low frustration tolerance. These findings are consistent with the idea that anxiety may impede the ability to tolerate everyday stressors, resulting in decreased coping (Gillott & Standen, 2007) and impeding the capacity of people with ASD to be resourceful and find solutions.

Solutions

The social interaction, communication, and cognitive impairments characteristic of ASD hinder the ability of individuals with ASD to generate effective intervention strategies during anxiety-provoking situations (Reaven & Hepburn, 2006). Therefore, individuals with ASD must be provided with strategies that are designed to promote adaptive behaviors involving techniques for self-calming, self-management, and self-awareness, thus preventing or decreasing the severity of maladaptive behavioral manifestations of anxious symptomology (Myles, 2003). However, to provide effective solutions, it is necessary first to obtain a deeper understanding of the experience of anxiety in affected individuals and the consequences of these feelings. Accurate identification of possible anxiety-provoking situations, signs, and symptoms, as well as potential predisposing and preventive factors, will be pertinent to the development and implementation of effective coping strategies for this population (Bellini, 2006; Reaven et al., 2009).

Empirically based intervention strategies designed specifically for individuals with ASD who experience anxiety are lacking (White et al., 2010). To illustrate, although cognitive behavioral therapy has been identified as a possible treatment for children with ASD, the results of such attempts have been mixed (Moree & Davis, 2010), and the implications for adults with ASD are unknown. One limitation of this approach may be the inability of some individuals with ASD to institute the necessary cognitive strategies (e.g., identifying and challenging unhelpful thinking) while experiencing anxiety. Thus, researchers need to explore other possibilities, in particular, ways of preventing the onset of anxiety. The first step to developing effective solutions is to understand the phenomenology of anxiety from the firsthand perspective of individuals with ASD, as well as the perspectives of parents with adult sons or daughters with ASD, and professionals working to support their needs.

Method

Participants

Adults with ASD. The participants in the ASD group were 11 young adults with ASD (9 men, 2 women), between 18 and 35 years of age, who were recruited through the investigators' professional networks across metropolitan Victoria, Australia. Diagnoses were self-reported, and all participants were receiving relevant services for which a formal diagnosis of ASD was required. The ratio of males to females in the sample was broadly in keeping with that observed in the ASD population (Fombonne, 2009). All participants were verbal, and 10 contributed their views and experiences independently during the focus groups. In all, 1 participant contributed with the assistance of a family member, who supported his comprehension by explaining the questions asked of the group and elaborated on his brief comments to help relate his experiences to the group. A total of 3 participants attended community access and training programs, 5 were enrolled at universities, and 3 were unemployed at the time of the study.

Caregivers and professionals. The focus group for caregivers and professionals was composed of 10 adults: 3 women and 1 man who were parents of individuals with ASD, 5 women who were professionals working with clients with ASD, and 1 woman who was both a professional and parent of an adult with ASD. The parents and professionals were recruited through the investigators' networks across metropolitan Victoria.

Materials

The two focus groups were audio recorded and video recorded to assist with transcription and analysis. Transcriptions were made using Microsoft Word™.

Focus Groups

The two focus groups (parents and professionals first) were conducted 2 weeks apart at the Olga Tennison Autism Research Centre at La Trobe University, and were facilitated by the fourth and first authors, respectively. Each group lasted approximately 120 min, including a 15-min break in the middle. At the start of each group, the facilitator reiterated information contained in a Participant Information Sheet (distributed during recruitment) regarding the purpose of the group, the procedures that would be followed, and the fact that participants were allowed to withdraw at any time without question. To this end, the facilitators explained that if any participant felt anxious during the group, he or she could simply choose to leave the room. The participants were encouraged to say as little or as much as they liked and to raise any issues that they felt were pertinent. Participants also were encouraged to express their views and experiences through writing and drawing if they felt more comfortable doing so than talking within the group.

Each facilitator outlined a set of rules governing the group discussions focused on ensuring that (a) each person had an opportunity to express his or her views and experiences, (b) each person's comments would be respected, and (c) participants understood that the comments that others made in the group must not be repeated outside the group to maintain confidentiality. A semistructured interview guide was used to ensure that a range of issues were discussed, including (a) triggers of anxiety in young adults with ASD (situations that elicit anxiety), (b) consequences (what happens when anxiety has been triggered), and (c) solutions (what helps young adults with ASD manage their anxiety). In addition to these topics, the parents and professionals also were asked to talk about the impact that supporting young adults with ASD and anxiety had on their lives and the lives of others.

Analysis

The focus group transcripts and the written information provided by participants were analyzed using thematic analysis, as outlined by Braun and Clarke (2006). This method involves repeated cycles of analysis across six stages, using the constant comparative method (Creswell, 2007), leading to an abstract account of participant experiences, and it constitutes a rigorous qualitative method in its own right (Braun & Clarke, 2006). First, the focus group transcripts and the written information were read to facilitate familiarity with the contents.

Line-by-line analysis of the transcripts and written words was then undertaken to identify discrete ideas, incidents, and events in the data, which were assigned preliminary codes. A comment, for example, in which one participant spoke of the anxiety he experienced when explaining his diagnosis to others was assigned the code "sharing diagnosis." Similar and related codes were grouped into potential categories, from which themes emerged. To illustrate, the theme "disappointment" emerged to account for many different "triggers" of anxiety, which arose from situations in which participants felt strongly disappointed. Finally, each theme was systematically assessed to determine the extent to

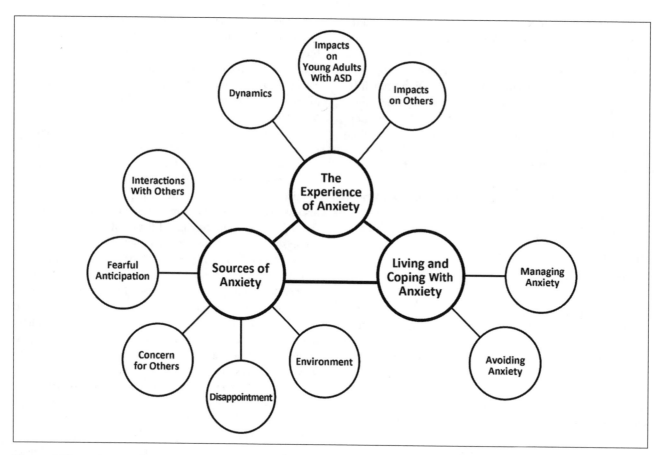

Figure 1. Thematic map of anxiety experiences.

which it accounted for the participants' experiences and its relationship to other themes expressed using a thematic map (Braun & Clarke, 2006) as outlined in Figure 1.

To help ensure credibility of the findings, the codes and themes identified by the first author were reviewed by the second author to identify errors or misinterpretations in the coding. Differences regarding interpretation were resolved through discussion and amended accordingly. In addition, the relevant guidelines for conducting qualitative research outlined by Chiovitti and Piran (2003) were adhered to, including (a) where possible, using the participants' own words to create the codes and themes, (b) identifying the basis on which the participants were selected, (c) specifying the aims of the research and locations where the study was carried out, and (d) describing how professional literature relates to the themes identified.

Results

A total of 3 themes and 10 subthemes emerged to account for the participants' everyday experiences of anxiety. As illustrated in Figure 1, the 3 main themes related directly to the participants' (a) sources (triggers) of anxiety, (b) experiences

of anxiety (consequences), and (c) strategies they had developed for living and coping with anxiety (solutions). The 3 themes, together with their subthemes, are presented using the participants' own words.

Sources of Anxiety

The young adults with ASD identified 20 sources of anxiety arising from everyday situations, whereas the parents and professionals identified 16. As presented in Table 1, 15 of the 20 sources were common across both groups. In addition, each of the young adults reported that he or she experienced multiple sources of anxiety. Through exploring the origin and nature of these sources of anxiety, five subgroupings emerged: (a) the environment, (b) interactions with others, (c) concern for others, (d) fearful anticipation of an event or outcome, and (e) disappointment. Pseudonyms are used in reporting the findings.

Immediate environment. According to the young adults with ASD, their everyday physical environments produced multiple sources of anxiety. Luke, for example, spoke of his fear of germs in his environment and the impact this fear had on his everyday life.

Table 1. Anxiety Sources, Experiences, and Strategies for Coping With Anxiety

Source, experiences, strategies	Young adults with ASD	Parents and professionals
Sources	Sound and light sensitivities	Lack of sleep
	Crowds	Crowds
	Uncertainty/making decisions	Uncertainty/making decisions
	Delays (e.g., transport)	Delays (e.g., transport)
	Anticipation and disappointment	Anticipation and disappointment
	Unexpected or sudden change	Unexpected or sudden change
	Health concerns (germs)	Health concerns (self and others)
	Public speaking	Public speaking
	Communicating with others	Communicating with others
	Perceived injustice to self or others	Tone of voice
	Authority (e.g., police, security)	Radio station not playing song
	News reports and other media	News reports and other media
	Meeting deadlines	Meeting deadlines
	Making eye contact	Ambiguous/open questions
	Losing things	Understanding social etiquette
	Bullying and gossip	
	Managing finances	
	Perceived surveillance of self	
	Explaining diagnosis	
	Life transition (e.g., leaving school)	
Experiences	Increased heart rate	Emotional (e.g., crying, screaming)
	Sweating	Challenging and repetitive behavior
	Obsessive thoughts/behavior	Obsessive thoughts/behavior
	Emotional (e.g., crying, screaming)	Emotional (e.g., crying, screaming)
	Frustration	Frustration
	Nausea	Humiliation
	Distraction	
Strategies	Listening to music	Heart rate monitors
	Singing	Allowing extra travel time
	Watching movies or TV	Watching movies or TV
	Developing multiple interests	Online learning
	Alternative therapies	Alternative therapies
	Study social skills resources	Humor
	Sleep	Mood monitor (visual chart)
	Exercise (walk, swim, run)	Exercise (walk, swim, run)
	Journaling	Journaling
	Looking at pictures	Looking at pictures
	Withdrawal (physically/mentally)	Withdrawal (physically/mentally)
	Talking with trusted person	Talking with trusted person
	Riding motorbike	
	Self-talk	
	Deep breathing and meditation	
	Online social networking	
	Computer games	
	Drugs and alcohol	

There isn't really a physical surface in the world that I'm not scared of—there isn't anywhere that I'm not scared—it just makes me feel angry and powerless and nauseous wherever I go and whatever I do.

Shane, on the other hand, spoke of the anxiety caused by the sensory environment he had to navigate in going about everyday tasks such as traveling to the university.

I get pissed off when I'm on the train in the morning and all the students get on and are talking and talking, and I'm in an enclosed area, and sometimes the fluorescents [lights] are flickering, and I'm like "No, no."

Shane went on to explain that crowded environments, such as university lecture halls and tutorial rooms, were also a source of anxiety, a sentiment shared by Brian: *"Crowded buses, that makes me anxious too."* Indeed, most young adults with ASD identified interacting with other people, whether on a crowded bus or a one-to-one conversation, as a key source of anxiety.

Interactions with others. Shane described the sources and feelings of anxiety that arose for him in interacting with other people as part of his university education. This included the anxiety associated with his attempts to adapt his communication style to meet the styles of others without ASD.

I'm a very blunt and direct person but apparently the people in my course, they get offended when I'm being honest. [They tell me that.] I have to use white lies and I have to talk in a more indirect manner. So then I have anxiety about how to talk in a more indirect manner and how to appeal to their "emotions" and how to sound "flowery" and "pleasant."

Shane went on to speak about the difficulties associated with adapting his communication style, including the physical and emotional tension: *"I can only do that for a certain amount of time each day and I get burnt-out talking to people."*

Melissa also noted that attempting to adapt to the communication styles of others, in this case through making eye contact, was a key source of anxiety: *"I actually get quite anxious with [having to make] eye contact."*

Andrew said that he felt anxious, distracted, and at times "paranoid" during interactions because he felt his behavior was constantly being watched and judged by him and others.

It feels as though I've got a surveillance, [a] video camera in my head, watching my every move and it's basically judging me, saying, "Why the hell are you doing this? Why the hell are you doing that? You should've done it this way or that way."

Andrew's comments were echoed by Brian who reported that he became anxious in situations where he felt he was being watched by others. *"[I feel anxious] when someone looks over my shoulder for no reason."*

Consistent with these reports, the parents and professionals identified interactions with others as a key source of anxiety for young adults with ASD. Linda, for example,

explained that the manner in which high school teachers talk with young adults with ASD can trigger anxiety.

So, in the senior school, some of the students can be provoked quite easily, even if the teacher is trying to help the clients comprehend, even adjusting tone of voice and things like that. And, if their tone is too aggressive, then the students will become extremely anxious.

Similarly, Susan noted that young adults with ASD may become anxious if they have difficulty comprehending what is said in a conversation.

You know, two or three members of the family get together and they forget that my son is only really picking up half of the conversation and it's invariably the wrong half. And things that he will then sense as a threat to some things being changed or whatever. So, those threats really come through, I think, quite strongly in everyday life—increasing his levels of arousal.

Fitting in with these observations was a consensus among the participants in both groups that communication partners (i.e., other participants in the interaction) play a key role in mediating the anxiety experiences of young adults with ASD.

Concern for others. In addition to feeling anxious in their interactions with others, the young adults with ASD expressed feeling anxious out of concern for others and their communities at large. To illustrate, Shane expressed concern and suspicion that people are being misled, to their detriment, by politicians: *"I get very anxious about how the parliaments, they do policies only to sway people to vote for them and not because it genuinely benefits society."* Jennifer expressed similar concern, explaining that she felt anxious about a recent change in the government and had deep concerns about perceived injustices in society.

I become anxious about politics—the government doing things wrong—partially and especially about people being oppressed. I can't stop thinking about it, I can't focus on good things, and it exhausts me. I was relieved when [the election] was finally over!

Shane's and Jennifer's comments were consistent with the reports of the parents and professionals, who also identified having "concern for others" as a key source of anxiety among some young adults with ASD. Victoria, for example, noted that after hearing media reports, her adult son had become very concerned about the 12-year drought that was occurring at the time of the study and its impact on others: *"[He is] stressing about the environment and [asking] are we getting enough rain? He is checking the water meter every day."* Victoria then went on to explain that her son had also become anxious out of concern for others after hearing media reports regarding the effects of smoking, eventually losing his job as a direct result of the anxiety.

[He is also] concerned about people smoking in that he is worried for their health because I've had to stop him say "Smoking is a health hazard" to them all the time. You know, because he was concerned. In fact, he lost a job because he was so upset that other people were smoking near him.

Fearful anticipation. Both groups of participants identified anticipation as a key source of anxiety. Peter, for example, said that he feels anxious about the future.

I've been unemployed probably for 7 years—with the global financial crisis and all that, it's been hard for a lot of people to get work—not just me. And I hate volunteering—I mean, I need money to survive. So for me, what makes me anxious is just what will happen in the future, the uncertainty of it all, I guess.

Shane, on the other hand, said he quickly became anxious when a situation arose in which he might need to speak in front of others.

I get anxiety when I have to talk in public, like . . . for example, if the lecturer finishes a lecture and says "Does anyone have questions?" and I have a question, my heart starts beating faster. Whenever my heart beats faster, I get anxious.

Susan, a parent, however, spoke more broadly about the types of situations that may lead to anxiety, before proving specific examples.

Anything that he's anticipating should happen or could happen or he would like to happen, and doesn't. For example, someone not replying to an e-mail immediately and radio stations not playing the right songs or they're missing out on playing one song from the 60s, at least one an hour—those sorts of things, the fine, minute [details] tied up with his obsessions.

Similarly, Stuart, a professional who worked in a university, spoke of the generalized sense of anxiety experienced by many students with ASD at the start of each academic year due to a desire to control unpredictability.

Something that triggers our students often is at the start of the year, at the start of the semester, selecting

your tutorials and your timetable causes anxiety, and that's anticipating or wanting something to be put in place, and it's an unknown because they might get that tutorial, but they might not.

Disappointment. The final source of anxiety identified by participants in both groups was disappointment. Brian explained that he often felt disappointed and became anxious when public transport did not arrive on time: *"Trains being late—5 min [late]."*

Andrew, on the other hand, who was interested in cricket, explained that the disappointment associated with his team losing was a key source of anxiety: *"I used to get anxious about Australia winning and that sort of thing."* Both Andrew and Victoria, who was a parent of a young adult with ASD, noted that the anxiety experienced as a result of sporting disappointment was different to that which might be experienced by a devoted sporting fan: *"Especially at the football, if his team doesn't win, although I have no control of it and [my son] has no control of it, I am somehow held accountable."*

The analysis revealed that the experiences of anxiety among young adults with ASD are complex, often difficult, but certainly painful and debilitating, and that the impacts of anxiety are often felt well beyond the specific situation in which it originates. It was through this process that the theme "the experience of anxiety" emerged.

The Experience of Anxiety: Dissociation and Dislocation

The young adults with ASD provided rich accounts of their personal experiences of anxiety, with similarities and differences across the group in relation to the dynamics of anxiety (e.g., onset, course) and its impact on their lives. These reports were echoed by parents and professionals, based on their observations of young adults with ASD, resulting in two subthemes—dynamics and impacts on young adults with ASD—described next. The parents and professionals also noted the impact of anxiety on people around young adults with ASD, including family and members of the public, leading to the emergence of a third subtheme, "impacts on others."

Dynamics. Some participants, including Luke, described the experience of anxiety as unavoidable with a sudden onset.

It's entirely circumstantial—mine's pretty much circumstantial so, you know, as soon as I see . . . as soon as something happens that upsets me, it's instantaneous—BANG! Like a bucket of cold water to the face.

However, other participants, including Ben, described a more gradual onset:

I find that it builds up, it doesn't just happen like an explosion—it, ah, sort of one thing might trigger it, get it rolling, and then, something else might crop up um that might cause me to get a little bit more anxious like losing stuff.

Either way, most of the young adults indicated that once triggered, their feelings of anxiety tended to grow as they became increasingly aware of the inexorable panic and their own reaction to it, as Jennifer explained.

Sometimes, anxiety can build up on itself like a brick on an accelerator pedal; whenever you make a mistake due to anxiety, you become more anxious. It's just something that keeps being in your head and you can't get it out and you can't focus on other things.

Impacts on young adults with ASD. The participants said that they were aware of their anxiety and described physiological signs, including increased heart rate, sweating, and nausea, as Melissa's comment illustrates:

I get heaviness in the center of my chest and I start getting very, very hot and the more anxious I am, the more difficult it is for me to get my ideas into words— either written or verbal.

As Melissa noted, anxiety not only resulted in a range of physiological signs but also had a real impact on her ability to engage in everyday activities. Indeed, the impact of anxiety on everyday activities was emphasized by participants in the parents and professionals group also. The parents and professionals were unanimous in their concerns regarding the impact of anxiety on the participation of young adults with ASD in everyday activities. Stuart, for example, noted that anxiety can act as a barrier to young adults accessing higher education: *"They get removed from the situation or they remove themselves—They just can't participate."* Similarly, Emma noted the impact that anxiety has on her adult daughter's ability to communicate with others:

With my daughter, probably one of the main things that happens in stressful situations is that she gets flustered, she loses the ability to really say what she wants or thinks or what she has to say. If given time, she'll calm down herself but, mostly, she tends to withdraw from the situation rather than engage.

The parents and professionals also raised concerns regarding the impact that anxiety can have on the way others perceive young adults with ASD, noting that this is a further barrier to participation in everyday activities.

Impacts on others. The key concern raised by parents and professionals was that people often misinterpret the anxiety-related behavior of young adults with ASD. To illustrate, Stuart spoke of an experience when a high school student became anxious and upset, leading to humiliation for that person:

One student becomes very, very verbose and emotional and scares people around her. If people aren't aware of her or her behavior, security might be called. So there is a lot of potential humiliation, but people then make assumptions about this behavior that may not be true or accurate. And that's unfortunate.

Parents also noted that knowing their son or daughter may have difficulties in particular situations due to anxiety created uncertainty for them, as Victoria explained.

I am aware that my son does a lot of transport by himself and I send him off into the world because there is no way I can keep him at home because he would become too frustrated. So, he goes off into the world and I just have to hope that if anyone approaches him, he'll run away rather than try and converse with them, because that's when the situation arises. But I have had phone calls from the police worried about whether I knew where he was and, generally, I don't know where he is, but I know roughly where he is, and they've been satisfied with my responses that he's OK but, obviously, people have called the police and I think they've been worried about what he was doing—I think.

There was consensus across both groups that the development and use of practical strategies played a key role in addressing the sources, experiences, and impacts of anxiety in everyday life for young adults with ASD, and for exploring new solutions.

Living and Coping With Anxiety

The young adults with ASD, and the parents and professionals identified strategies for preventing and managing anxiety that they had used themselves, would like to use, or had observed. The parents and professionals focused on strategies aimed at preventing the onset of anxiety, whereas the young adults tended to focus on strategies to manage the anxiety once it had occurred. Two subthemes, "preventing anxiety" and "managing anxiety," are presented next.

Preventing anxiety. For Emma, a parent, a key strategy for helping her daughter avoid anxiety was to be organized.

She gets stressed if she's running late for anything. [Therefore], we try to make sure she gets there in plenty of time. If she has an 11 a.m. lecture, she'll head off at 20 min to 11 a.m. to make sure that she is there on time.

Claire used another strategy, feeling that her adult son benefited from a regular exercise program that helped to not only manage but also reduce his anxiety due to its predictability.

[He] has a program at the gym, such as 12 repetitions on one exercise, 10 min, on that so there are a lot of number sequences behind the program. I've noticed, over time, there's a little bit of diminished anxiety because of the consistency of exercise.

Shane, a young adult with ASD, explained that he was trying to avoid anxiety by learning strategies for interacting with people without ASD:

I read social skills books and "Yahoo Answers" on what people regard as polite, and I try to copy that. So, to me, it's rote memory. It doesn't come to me naturally. I have to manually learn it, and people have to specifically teach me what is considered polite. I don't know it naturally, so I feel very robotic when I talk to neurotypicals.

Despite the use of these proactive strategies, the vast majority of strategies identified by young adults with ASD focused on managing existing anxiety.

Managing anxiety. The most common strategy for managing anxiety was to escape, either physically or through diversion and distraction. *"I've got some strategies [for dealing with anxiety]. I go for a walk or run. I wish I could literally run to the hills."* Music was another commonly identified de-stressor, as Andrew noted, *"I find listening to music on my iPod to be really helpful. If I am really down and depressed and in the dumps, I'll start listening to a series of songs."*

Retreat into the comfort of other technologies provided frequent respite also. Melissa, for example, identified a computer game that she liked to play to manage her anxiety in addition to escaping and listening to music.

With me, there are probably three main things which help me calm down: (1) my music, (2) removing myself from what is the trigger—either physically or emotionally somehow, and (3) fiddling—say, knitting or something. However, [computer company] has this really good game, which I enjoy. It usually gets all those three things (mentioned above) in one go. It's a game where you're patting fish, basically. It's a very basic, very simple game. It removes me from the stress triggers and it has the music going for it.

Similarly, Luke noted that he found computer games offered a distraction from feeling anxious: *"I lose myself in computer games because it's something linear, it's something that you don't have to devote all your thoughts at once to and dealing with neurotypicals."*

Other participants, including Brian, reported that listening to music and relaxation techniques were effective in managing anxiety: *"Go for a walk, take some deep breaths, listen to music, relax in your bedroom."*

Several participants, including Luke, spoke of the benefits associated with talking with other people who understand what it is like to have ASD and experience anxiety.

Sometimes talking about your stressful situation with other people who are familiar with, with you. Neurotypicals probably aren't recommended, except for your parents, but if you're talking about someone who has it, you know, you can sort things out, you calm down a little bit.

Andrew suggested that social networking sites, through which he can communicate with other people with similar experiences without the pressures associated with face-to-face communication, were helpful.

I've found that with a lot of people on the spectrum are using social networking sites to, ah, sort of keep them in contact with other people without—you know—being in the comfort of their own home without having to go out and into public, open environment and socialize face-to-face. For example, I talk on Skype with various mates of mine and I also find that that really helps.

Ben suggested that it would be helpful to have a support line available specifically to adults with ASD, where they could access support from trained professionals. *"It would be cool if there was a hotline specifically for people with autism, particularly if they're feeling stressed. Have a counselor on the other end of the line."*

Several participants had learned strategies for managing anxiety from professionals and friends. Jennifer described the strategies she had been taught by her psychologist: *"My psychologist taught me to get grounded, to concentrate on what I can see, hear, smell, taste, and feel inside and outside my body."* Andrew explained a method his friend had taught him: *"One of my mates has taught me to just treat it like it's not an important thing, that it doesn't matter if you're not perfect all the time. That sort of stuff."*

Only one participant, whose pseudonym identity has also been withheld for additional privacy, reported using drugs and alcohol in the past in an attempt to manage anxiety.

I feel anxious. Like at parties, I feel very uncomfortable, so I have to drink lots of alcohol. I also tried marijuana because someone gave it to me as a birthday present and that actually reduced my anxiety, but it is illegal and, also, I don't have access to it anymore so, yeah, but that's not in Australia.

A complete list of the strategies for living and coping with anxiety identified by the participants in both groups is presented in Table 1.

Discussion

Our aim in this study was to explore the everyday experiences of young adults with ASD based on their firsthand experiences, and the reports of parents and professionals who support them. The results clearly demonstrate that anxiety affects the lives of young adults with ASD and the individuals around them. The results also demonstrate that the sources of anxiety, the symptoms and experience of anxiety, and the strategies young adults with ASD use to manage anxiety are highly individualized. The implications of these preliminary findings for clinical practice and future research directions are discussed with regard to the existing literature.

Understanding the Sources of Anxiety

The young adults with ASD reported difficulties with social interactions (e.g., "small talk"), which are inherent to ASD, and performance anxiety (e.g., public speaking) as key sources of anxiety, consistent with the findings of Bellini (2006) in his study of adolescents with ASD. In addition, the participants reported that environmental noise, health concerns, unexpected change, and disappointment also were key sources of anxiety. The fact that unexpected change, disappointment, and environmental noise were identified as triggers suggests that the relationship between key characteristics of ASD and anxiety may extend beyond the impact of social impairment, as previously reported in the literature. That is, other ASD-related characteristics, such as sensory aversions and a strong desire for routine and sameness, also may be implicated. Either way, the fact that each participant identified a unique set of multiple sources indicates that a "one size fits all" approach to supporting young adults with ASD is unlikely to be successful. Nevertheless, given that the young adults with ASD, parents, and professionals identified essentially the same sources, the results may provide a starting point for beginning to address these sources through tailored interventions.

An important finding of this study relates to the clear concern that young adults with ASD expressed for others and society at large, to the extent that it was a source of anxiety for many of them. Shane and Jennifer, for example, expressed concern that other people were being misled by politicians and, more broadly, about injustice in society. Victoria reported that her adult son was very anxious about rainfall and the environment, and that he had lost his job due to expressing concern for people who were smoking outside his workplace after watching an antismoking campaign on TV. The fact that young adults with ASD are concerned about others and society at large should not come as a surprise, but it has rarely been documented in the ASD literature. The results suggest that any attempts to help young adults with ASD manage their anxiety must address inward and outward sources of anxiety while acknowledging that some outward sources, such as the health and political choices of others, cannot be controlled.

Experiences of Anxiety

Irrespective of the sources of anxiety, the participants' reports of the emotional and physical consequences were compelling. Participants spoke of feeling frustrated, depressed, withdrawn, and robotic while experiencing racing heartbeats, sweating, and nausea. Although previous researchers (e.g., Reaven & Hepburn, 2006) have documented these symptoms in regard to children with ASD, the present findings can be used to extend the scope of study to young adults with ASD, and they highlight the consequences on their lives and the lives of others. That is, the participants in this study reported that anxiety represented not only an emotional or physical state but also a key barrier to their participation in everyday activities, such as using public transport, meeting with friends, and attending school.

The participants' comments indicate that the dynamics of anxiety—including onset and escalation—differ for each person. Luke, for example, described a sudden onset like a "bucket of cold water to the face," whereas other participants described a more gradual roller coaster. Several participants, as well as parents and professionals, emphasized the fluctuating nature of anxiety that makes predicting how an individual may feel or cope in a specific situation on any given day difficult. The parents, in particular, said that these fluctuations made it hard to plan and provide support; thus, it appears to be a source of caregiver burden. Nevertheless, all participants indicated that they had insight into their own level of anxiety, or anxiety in others, in the case of parents, and had identified strategies for living and coping with it accordingly.

Living and Coping With Anxiety

The participants identified a range of strategies for living and coping with anxiety, including withdrawing, relaxing, and exercise. Of these, withdrawing from anxiety-inducing situations to a context or place in which the triggers are not present, or the people within that context will be understanding, was the most common strategy across participants. Several young adults with ASD spoke of escaping to online social networking sites where they could talk with others with ASD, or of immersing themselves in computer games, as ways of coping. Others said that they retreated to a quiet room, listened to music, watched movies, or exercised to escape. In contrast to these reactive strategies, far less emphasis was placed on preventing or preempting anxiety. It is not clear from the findings whether this is due to the inherent difficulties associated with trying to prevent the multiple sources of anxiety the participants reported or whether this reflects a preference for reactive strategies. Either way, the results provide clear evidence of the importance of coping strategies in the lives of young adults with ASD who experience anxiety and the people close to them.

Limitations and Opportunities

The results of this study can be used to extend the existing literature by documenting anxiety in this adult population of individuals with ASD, as opposed to children and adolescents, and by doing so through their own words as opposed to formal tools and measures. Nevertheless, given that qualitative researchers make no claims about generalization, the findings are limited to accounting for the experiences of the participants in the study. Future studies involving larger groups and a combination of quantitative and qualitative methods will further advance understanding of what is an important issue in the lives of young adults with ASD, their parents, and the professionals who support them. Such studies should include standardized measures of anxiety to get a better characterization of the anxiety symptoms experienced by participants, thus allowing for a more detailed analysis of these experiences as well as their strategies and outcomes.

The focus groups provided a forum in which participants could share and discuss their experiences and views freely, allowing them to present the issues most meaningful to them. In addition, the involvement of three different groups of participants (young adults with ASD, parents, and professionals) allowed for triangulation of the data. Focus groups involve social interaction in a semistructured environment, and some young adults with ASD may have been reluctant to participate or to express themselves fully during the study. In future studies, researchers could incorporate additional modes of data collection, such as one-to-one interviews, either face-to-face or online, in an attempt to ensure that methods employed do not deter full participation.

Future Research Directions

We interpret our findings to conclude that attempts to support young adults with ASD to live and cope with anxiety must address individual and environmental factors. There are opportunities to develop and evaluate practical approaches for making community and educational environments more accessible, such as working with universities to provide greater support to young adults with ASD at the time of enrollment and reducing unnecessary public speaking requirements in classes. Similarly, there are opportunities to develop and evaluate new technologies that may help young adults with ASD monitor and manage their anxiety. Fundamental to any approach, will be the need to (a) understand and address the social difficulties inherent in the disorder, (b) use existing treatments for clinical anxiety, where appropriate and to the greatest extent possible, and (c) ensure that young adults with ASD are partners in the process so that any solutions developed are relevant to and useful in their everyday lives. Indeed, we interpret the results as clearly demonstrating that young adults with ASD, along with their parents and the professionals who support them, are the best source of information and ideas for strategies.

Conclusion

The focus groups confirmed the reported research, which indicated high levels of anxiety among individuals with ASD. A novel aspect of this study was to approach the experience of anxiety in several ways: by examining triggers, consequences, and solutions, and through the views of the clients, their parents, and expert professionals. It is clear from this study (and related studies) that anxiety is caused by unexpected change, social encounters, and many other situations, but there is a lack of understanding as to solutions that may assist young adults with ASD cope with the anxiety. Our use of focus groups allowed the voices of the people intimately involved to be enunciated comprehensively. Qualitative data analysis complemented the process of elicitation of key concerns and issues, and it led to a description of five contexts for anxiety creation: external surroundings, personal interactions, concern for others, fearful anticipation, and serious disappointments. In further research, investigators could focus productively on the gamut of solutions suggested by the participants in this study.

Acknowledgments

We would like to express our sincere gratitude to the participants in this study who generously shared their experiences and insights. We also would like to acknowledge the contribution of our colleagues Michael Burnside, Elfriede Ihsen, Shonali Krishnaswamy, Seng Loke, and Wojciech Nadachowski whose mutual interest and work with us in this area helped to inform the study.

Authors' Note

This study was approved by the La Trobe University Faculty Human Research Ethics Committee.

Declaration of Conflicting Interests

The author(s) declared no potential conflicts of interest with respect to the research, authorship, and/or publication of this article.

Funding

The author(s) received no financial support for the research, authorship, and/or publication of this article.

References

American Psychiatric Association. (2000). *Diagnostic and statistical manual of mental disorders* (4th ed., text rev.). Washington, DC: Author.

Bellini, S. (2004). Social skill deficits and anxiety in high-functioning adolescents with autism spectrum disorders. *Focus on Autism and Other Developmental Disabilities, 19*, 78–86.

Bellini, S. (2006). The development of social anxiety in adolescents with autism spectrum disorders. *Focus on Autism and Other Developmental Disabilities, 21*, 138–145.

Braun, V., & Clarke, V. (2006). Using thematic analysis in psychology. *Qualitative Research in Psychology, 3*, 77–101.

Chiovitti, R. F., & Piran, N. (2003). Methodological issues in nursing research: Rigour and grounded theory research. *Journal of Advanced Nursing, 44*, 427–435.

Creswell, J. W. (2007). *Qualitative enquiry and research design: Choosing among five approaches* (2nd ed.). Thousand Oaks, CA: SAGE.

Drahota, A. M. (2009). Intervening with independent daily living skills for high-functioning children with autism and concurrent anxiety disorders. *Dissertation Abstracts International Section A: Humanities and Social Sciences, 69*(7A), 2601.

Evans, D. W., Canavera, K., Kleinpeter, F. L., Maccubbin, E., & Taga, K. (2005). The fears, phobias, and anxieties of children with autism spectrum disorders and Down syndrome: Comparisons with developmentally and chronologically age matched children. *Child Psychiatry & Human Development, 36*, 3–26.

Fombonne, E. (2009). Epidemiology of pervasive developmental disorders. *Pediatric Research, 65*, 591–598.

Gillott, A., Furniss, F., & Walter, A. (2001). Anxiety in high-functioning children with autism. *Autism, 5*, 277–286.

Gillott, A., & Standen, P. J. (2007). Levels of anxiety and sources of stress in adults with autism. *Journal of Intellectual Disabilities, 11*, 359–370.

Gresham, F. M., & Elliot, S. N. (1990). *Social Skills Rating System*. Circle Pines, MN: American Guidance Service.

Grover, R. L., Ginsburg, G. S., & Ialongo, N. (2005). Childhood predictors of anxiety symptoms: A longitudinal study. *Child Psychiatry & Human Development, 36*, 133–153.

Kim, J. A., Szatmari, P., Bryson, S. E., Streiner, D. L., & Wilson, F. J. (2000). The prevalence of anxiety and mood problems among children with autism and Asperger syndrome. *Autism, 4*, 117–132.

La Greca, A. M. (1999). *Social Anxiety Scales for children and adolescents*. Miami, FL: University of Miami.

March, J. S. (1999). *Multidimensional Anxiety Scale for children*. North Tonawanda, NY: Multi-Health Systems.

Moree, B. N., & Davis, T. E. (2010). Cognitive-behavioral therapy for anxiety in children diagnosed with autism spectrum disorders: Modification trends. *Research in Autism Spectrum Disorders, 4*, 346–354.

Myles, B. S. (2003). Behavioral forms of stress management for individuals with Asperger syndrome. *Child and Adolescent Psychiatric Clinics of North America, 12*, 123–141.

Reaven, J., Blakeley-Smith, A., Nichols, S., Dasari, M., Flanigan, E., & Hepburn, S. (2009). Cognitive-behavioral group treatment for anxiety symptoms in children with high-functioning autism spectrum disorders: A pilot study. *Focus on Autism and Other Developmental Disabilities, 24*, 27–37.

Reaven, J., & Hepburn, S. (2006). The parent's role in the treatment of anxiety symptoms in children with high-functioning autism spectrum disorders. *Mental Health Aspects of Developmental Disabilities, 9*(3), 73–80.

Spence, S. H. (1995). Social skills training: Enhancing social competence and children and adolescents. Windsor, UK: The NFER-NELSON Publishing Company Ltd.

Spence, S. H. (1997). *Spence Children's Anxiety Scale (parent version)*. Brisbane, Australia: University of Queensland.

White, S., Albano, A., Johnson, C. L., Kasari, C., Ollendick, T., Klin, A., & Scahill, L. (2010). Development of a cognitive-behavioral intervention program to treat anxiety and social deficits in teens with high-functioning autism. *Clinical Child and Family Psychology Review, 13*, 77–90.

White, S., Oswald, D., Ollendick, T., & Scahill, L. (2009). Anxiety in children and adolescents with autism spectrum disorders. *Clinical Psychology Review, 29*, 216–229.

HAMMILL INSTITUTE
ON DISABILITIES

Focus on Autism and Other
Developmental Disabilities
27(4) 225–236
© 2012 Hammill Institute on Disabilities
Reprints and permission:
sagepub.com/journalsPermissions.nav
DOI: 10.1177/1088357612460274
http://foa.sagepub.com

SAGE

Using Transfer of Stimulus Control Technology to Promote Generalization and Spontaneity of Language

Trina D. Spencer, PhD[1] and Thomas S. Higbee, PhD[2]

Abstract

Children with autism often use newly acquired language in restricted contexts and with limited variability. Instructional tactics that embed generalization technology have shown promise for increasing spontaneity, response variation, and the generalized use of language across settings, people, and materials. In this study, we explored the integration of textual scripts and explicit engineering of transfer of stimulus control procedures to facilitate functional conversation skills of a young girl with autism. The generalized use of prepositions, coordinating conjunctions, and subordinating conjunctions was assessed within the context of natural conversation with teachers, parents, and peers. The intentional programming of training contexts has the potential to affect language spontaneity, generalization, and variability without relying on script-fading conventions.

Keywords

script training, generalization, language, autism, conversation

Significant language deficits and impaired social interactions are characteristics of children with autism (American Psychiatric Association, 2000). Many children with autism display limited spontaneity and generalization of newly acquired language skills (Carr & Kologinsky, 1983; Charlop, Schreibman, & Thibodeau, 1985; Koegel, 2000) and engage socially only in response to questions or prompts from adults and in tightly controlled training environments (Chiang & Carter, 2008; Sigafoos & Reichle, 1993). For example, a child with autism may talk only about his/her current activity when directly asked about it, and after several training sessions. In contrast, typically developing children seek out friends, initiate conversations with questions or comments, and use language appropriate for the immediate context.

For language skills to be functional, their use needs to become spontaneous, to occur in a variety of nontraining situations, and to extend beyond directly taught statements. Spontaneity is typically discussed with respect to specific programmed or unprogrammed antecedent stimuli that prompt targeted language behaviors. Instead, spontaneity could be conceived as the extent to which naturally occurring conversational contexts contain the discriminative stimuli that evoke language use (Carter & Hotchkis, 2002; Sigafoos & Reichle, 1993). The degree of intrusiveness of the controlling stimuli or the salience of contextual events also is relevant. The less obvious and intrusive the

discriminative stimuli, the more spontaneous the response may be considered (Halle, 1987). For example, language evoked by a conversation partner and the presence of toys is more spontaneous than language evoked by a teacher's vocal prompt because explicit prompting from adults is intrusive and does not occur in natural conversation. Training for spontaneity involves the careful arrangement of antecedent stimuli to promote the transfer of stimulus control from programmed stimuli such as adult prompting to unprogrammed stimuli such as the presence of toys and conversation partners (e.g., Argott, Townsend, Sturmey, & Poulson, 2008; Brown, Krantz, McClannahan, & Poulson, 2008; Krantz & McClannahan, 1993). This transfer of stimulus control occurs through a process of pairing the programmed stimuli (e.g., prompts) with antecedent stimuli that are typically present in the natural, nontraining environments. Gradual fading of the programmed stimuli can facilitate the transfer (Cooper, Heron, & Heward, 2007; Stokes & Baer, 1977).

[1]Northern Arizona University, Flagstaff, USA
[2]Utah State University, Logan, USA

Corresponding Author:
Trina D. Spencer, Northern Arizona University, P. O. Box 5630, Flagstaff, AZ 86011-5630, USA
Email: Trina.Spencer@nau.edu

Stimulus/situation generalization is assessed in much of the language research conducted with children with autism. This type of generalization involves the transfer of stimulus control of acquired skills from a set of stimuli present in the training environment (e.g., conversation partners and setting of interaction) to similar stimuli that were not present during training (Cooper et al., 2007; Stokes & Baer, 1977). For instance, a child who was taught to say, "Look" to a teacher sitting at a desk might later emit the response "Look" in the presence of a peer on the playground.

Another way to conceptualize generalization is by determining the degree of flexibility in the use of newly acquired language. Response generalization occurs when one response is taught and then, following training, the child emits one or more different but functionally equivalent responses (Cooper et al., 2007). For example, a child is taught, "Look what I can do" and later, without any direct training on response forms, he/she uses a different but functionally equivalent response such as, "Watch what I am doing." In response generalization, the antecedent stimuli present in the conversational context have control over a set of functionally equivalent responses or a response class, which might be a looser type of stimulus control than if they controlled only one specific response form.

Many children with autism require systematic and carefully engineered training programs before they experience significant generalization of behavior change (Koegel, 2000; McConnell, 2002). Often, training begins with the acquisition of new verbal responses and, following proficient use of those responses under controlled training conditions, the focus of training changes to pragmatics—spontaneity and generalization. In initial training, reinforcement of specific forms of language exclusively in the presence of programmed antecedent stimuli may hinder the transfer of stimulus control to nontraining antecedent stimuli and settings, and restrict response variations. Several researchers have noted that precise stimulus control desired during initial training with children with autism may interfere with the spontaneous and generalized use of the newly acquired verbal responses (Carr, 1982; Carr & Kologinsky, 1983; Sigafoos & Reichle, 1993). Given that children with autism may need systematic training to use language functionally and that narrow stimulus control can impair spontaneity and generalization, procedures that balance effective acquisition with the strategic transfer of stimulus control are needed.

One procedure that was designed to enhance the spontaneous and generalized use of language among children with autism is script training. To reduce the need for intrusive vocal prompting from adults, auditory or written phrases, managed by the child, are used to prompt targeted language utterances. Children are first taught to use scripts. This may involve pointing to and reading textual scripts or inserting cards through a Language Master® device and repeating the recorded message. Following initial script

training procedures, scripts are typically faded by gradually eliminating parts of the scripts (McClannahan & Krantz, 2005). Several researchers have investigated the effect of scripts and script fading on language skills of children with autism with varying degrees of success. In an early script intervention study, Krantz and McClannahan (1993) scripted 10 written statements or questions for participants to read during leisure activities with a peer. Once participants were proficient responders, textual scripts were faded from end to beginning in five steps. During training and script fading, participants made conversational statements cued by the scripts or the remaining element(s) of the scripts. All scripts were enclosed with a set of quotation marks (" "). The researchers conducted a series of stimulus/situation generalization sessions in a different room with a different teacher, at different times of day, and with different materials. With respect to response generalization, they measured unscripted initiations, which were defined as "verbal productions that differed from the script by more than conjunctions, articles, prepositions, pronouns, or changes in verb tense," (p. 124). Researchers programmed several features into the procedures to facilitate response variation. For example, scripts were developed to reflect recent or upcoming events and familiar school objects. Three different versions of scripts were created by randomly assigning the position of scripts before presenting them.

The results of this study were favorable as unscripted responses increased substantially and stimulus/situation generalization was achieved; however, when the scripts were faded completely, participants were unable to initiate conversation. The presence of the beginning quotation mark was necessary to evoke conversation. It is interesting to consider that, although quotation marks are not necessarily natural antecedent stimuli that typically control conversation, they are certainly less salient than the entire text script used in training. Moreover, the quotation marks, a nonspecific discriminative stimulus, cued speaking in general rather than specific statements. Given that the discriminative stimulus (i.e., the quotation marks) was useable for a variety of potential scripts appropriate for the conversational context, the outcome is significant.

Subsequently, Brown et al. (2008) supplemented script training and script-fading procedures with additional strategies to enhance the transfer of stimulus control of verbal responses to naturally occurring stimuli. They taught participants nine conversation statements that corresponded to nine items commonly found in convenience stores, sporting good stores, and video stores. Textual scripts were attached to these items during mock store training, and once participants responded proficiently using the scripts, scripts were faded from end to beginning in seven steps. Pre- and posttests were conducted in community stores and results indicated that participants emitted substantially more unprompted and unscripted interactions following script training and fading. Several features of their procedures facilitated natural environment stimulus control of conversational interactions. First, a subset of nine generalization stimuli was present during training; thus, multiple common stimuli were present during training and generalization settings. Second, the location of attached textual scripts on training stimuli was changed after each fading step. Third, manual prompting for participants to point to the script was provided only after 30 s of no talking, and the conversation partners never began the interactions. Fourth, adult conversation partners responded to participants' attempts to interact with natural conversation responses, making conversation responses a natural consequence of participants' initiations.

Although previous researchers supplemented script fading with various instructional arrangements to enhance spontaneity and generalization, the effort and duration of script fading was still significant (e.g., 5–7 steps over 16–52 sessions). Consequently, Woods and Poulson (2006) used a script training procedure without script fading to teach children with autism to initiate interactions with typically developing peers during art and play activities. Participants were prompted manually to use a binder filled with several textual scripts to cue initiations to peers. Although they were never faded during the training condition, scripts were not present during probe "lunch bunch" sessions. A variation of fading was accomplished by periodically exposing children to a similar context but without the scripts. When scripts were introduced, participants' scripted initiations increased significantly. During setting generalization probe sessions, initiations increased over baseline conditions, although they did not reach the level of initiations when scripts were present. Even though only moderate improvements in the generalization setting were noted, this outcome is important because it was accomplished in just a few training sessions (i.e., 3–13) and without the difficult to manage script-fading phase. Spontaneous and generalized language produced in fewer sessions and with less instructor effort has significant practical implications.

Based on this awareness, we developed a number of hypotheses that led to the intentional integration of multiple strategies to enhance the transfer of stimulus control without requiring script fading that included the following:

Hypothesis 1: Introducing several scripts at the same time should prevent children from reverting to previously learned scripts and reduce the possibility that children can memorize each one exactly.

Hypothesis 2: Eliminating a performance criterion should reduce the inadvertent reinforcement of invariable responses.

Hypothesis 3: Including natural contingencies (e.g., social attention instead of edibles) and highly preferred activities during training should eliminate motivation as a confound.

Hypothesis 4: Increasing the salience of paired stimuli (making both visual) should improve the transfer of stimulus control potential between the intrusive programmed stimuli (i.e., scripts) and the natural stimuli (i.e., toys and conversation partner).

These hypotheses led the current study to explore the effect of supplementing script training with a number of strategies to promote generalization on the spontaneous and generalized use of complex language targets of a child with autism. Specifically, we were interested in knowing whether combining script training and generalization strategies during the acquisition phases would enhance the transfer of stimulus control and whether stimulus control could be transferred from scripts to more naturally occurring stimuli in the absence of formal script fading. We carefully arranged our teaching procedures to include the following generalization-enhancing tactics: (a) natural contingencies of reinforcement, (b) training multiple exemplars, (c) training loosely, and (d) programming common stimuli (Stokes & Baer, 1977).

Method

Participant and Setting

Fran, a 5-year-old girl served as the participant in this study. At the time of the study, Fran attended a university-based preschool program with seven other preschool-age children. The program serves as a training center for undergraduate and graduate students who provide one-on-one intensive behavioral intervention to young children with autism. Fran was diagnosed with autism by a pediatrician and the district school psychologist prior to her involvement in the university-based program. Fran's mother described her as "high functioning." In general, Fran exhibited average- to above-average cognitive skills but displayed significant behavior problems, such as tantrums and routine inflexibility. Fran had functionally adequate language skills (i.e., she used spoken language to communicate her basic wants and needs) and spontaneously produced short, simple sentences. However, she often omitted smaller words like "to" and "am." For instance, a transcribed language sample taken prior to the study documented that Fran said, "I making rainbow" and "I want be this one." Although Fran was able to communicate with understanding adults, such as her parents and teachers, peers were not especially responsive to Fran's attempts to communicate. Despite her interest in being with typically developing peers, Fran did not consistently maintain eye contact with them or initiate conversation on topics of interest to her peers. Most of Fran's conversations occurred with adults and were initiated by adults.

Of the eight children with autism in the program at the time, Fran was the only one who was interested in peers and could communicate sufficiently. Because she lacked a community of peers in this program, Fran was escorted twice a week to a campus day care program during "free play," where she was encouraged to interact socially with typically developing peers. To prepare her for kindergarten in a less-restrictive setting, Fran was an ideal candidate for a social communication intervention with an explicit focus on the generalized use of language.

During the course of her 5 days a week participation in the university-based preschool program, Fran worked with four instructors, each once or twice a week for 4 hr at a time. Fran's instructors were undergraduate students in psychology or communication sciences. Instructors received extensive training in applied behavior analysis and were closely supervised by doctoral candidates and the program's director. Research activities were integrated into Fran's typical instructional time every day during the summer before she entered kindergarten.

For research purposes, we taught Fran conversational language in the context of art. Painting and coloring were some of Fran's favorite activities and sitting at a table with a conversation partner provided an appropriate level of structure for training. In kindergarten, Fran had frequent opportunities to sit near peers during art class and kindergarten children typically talk about ongoing projects with peers. Training in this context prepared Fran for future social interactions in kindergarten.

The majority of sessions took place in the university-based preschool at a small table. Setting generalization probes were conducted in Fran's home at the dining room table and, at follow-up, in her mainstream kindergarten classroom at a large table during art class.

Dependent Variables

The dependent variable was selected based on Fran's social language needs. We used a language sample analysis to identify developmentally appropriate language features absent in Fran's conversations. Fran's language productions were recorded using a digital voice recorder during conversation with her instructor (constituted first three baseline assessment sessions). Following the recording of three 3-min language samples, Fran's productions during conversation were transcribed and carefully reviewed for language features that she did not use (Robertson, 2007). After analyzing transcripts of Fran's first three baseline assessment sessions, we identified three language features and specific words to target in this study: (a) prepositions *on, in,* and *with*; (b) coordinating conjunctions *and* and *but*; and (c) subordinating conjunctions *when* and *because*. The number of language targets Fran emitted during daily 3-min assessment sessions was the primary dependent measure.

Assessment transcripts also were examined to identify who initiated the conversation. During assessment sessions, the conversation partner waited 20 s to allow Fran time to begin the conversation. If she had not initiated the conversation within 20 s, the conversation partner started talking about his/her own artwork. Each assessment session was marked as Fran initiated or conversation partner initiated. Only 7 sessions (four daily assessment sessions and three generalization probes) constitute the baseline condition for this analysis and 43 sessions make up the training condition. Percentage of conversations initiated by Fran was calculated for baseline and intervention phases.

Each of Fran's uses of the target language features was analyzed with reference to the scripts we trained. Previous researchers have analyzed unprompted responses; however, in our data, all responses are considered unprompted because data were collected in a naturalistic context in the absence of prompts. Therefore, a more appropriate analysis involved the extent to which Fran varied her responses while still using the targeted language features (i.e., response generalization). To determine whether Fran used the target words in a generalized manner, we calculated the percentage of targets emitted after teaching that constituted untrained uses of the target language feature. We defined untrained uses as the inclusion of a target word in a phrase that shared no other words with the script phrases except articles and pronouns such as *the, a,* and *my.* For example, if the script we trained read "The colors are pretty *on* the paper" and Fran said, "I got paint *on* my fingers," this was considered an untrained use of the preposition *on.* The percentage of untrained uses of targets was calculated for each of the three language features.

Reliability

Within 2 hr of completing an assessment session, the instructor listened to the digital recording and transcribed Fran's conversational exchanges word for word, including grammatical errors and word deletions. When transcribing, the instructor stopped and replayed the recording or parts of the recording as many times as necessary to obtain a complete transcription. The instructor analyzed each transcript for the number of language targets and calculated separate scores for prepositions, coordinating conjunctions, and subordinating conjunctions. To examine the consistency of scoring, the first author reviewed 36% of the transcripts across all phases, including generalization probes, and calculated independent scores for prepositions, coordinating conjunctions, and subordinating conjunctions. Based on the three language features (i.e., prepositions, coordinating conjunctions, and subordinating conjunctions), each transcript contained three categories for calculating agreement or disagreement. Scoring agreement was calculated using the following formula: number of agreements divided by the number of agreements plus disagreements multiplied by 100%. Interscorer agreement across all three language features was 94% with three discrepancies for prepositions. Because these disagreements were with the word *on*, it is likely that they were missed due to oversight and not because there was disagreement regarding how to classify the word.

Independent Variable

The independent variable included two major components—script training without fading and transfer of stimulus control procedures. The transfer of stimulus control procedures (or strategies to promote generalization) involved the systematic arrangement of multiple exemplars during training and the use of stimuli common to the training and naturalistic assessment conditions. In addition, we intentionally trained the multiple exemplars loosely and incorporated natural contingencies of reinforcement in training and assessment contexts (Stokes & Baer, 1977). For this study, textual scripts prompted what to say, but the strategies to promote generalization were intentionally arranged to enhance the functional use of those statements.

Development of scripts. Visual programmed stimuli (i.e., written scripts) were selected with the intent to make the natural antecedent stimuli (i.e., table, conversation partner, and toys), which were visual, more salient in the pairing process. Although impaired significantly by limited social communication skills and restricted patterns of behavior, Fran had extensive experience with books and text. At the time of the study, she recognized many familiar words and quickly learned new words. Early decoding ability is not unusual for children with autism (Newman et al., 2007) and given that many children with autism are visual learners, text may have several advantages over other forms of response prompts (Quill, 1997).

Textual scripts were written to be applicable to all types of art materials used in the study. Script sheets consisted of 8½ × 11-inch cardstock on which five textual scripts (i.e., *multiple exemplars*) were typed in large print. For each language target (i.e., prepositions, coordinating conjunctions, subordinating conjunctions), a set of three script sheets was used, each with a different order of the same five scripts. In other words, there were five scripts (textual lines) for each of the three language targets (see Table 1), but they were printed in different orders creating three separate script sheets for each target.

Prepositions were introduced first and these scripts were created so that the later targets were not included. However, some coordinating conjunction scripts contained prepositions, and some subordinating conjunction scripts contained prepositions and coordinating conjunctions. "I love to paint **with** this" is an example of a preposition script; "I love to play **and** paint *with* you" is an example of a coordinating conjunction script; "I love to paint *with* you **because** you're fun" and "It's messy **when** I get it *on* my hands *and* fingers" are examples of subordinating conjunction scripts. In these examples, the current targets are boldfaced and the previous targets are italicized. We created the scripts so that, once a new target was introduced, Fran continued to receive some exposure to previously learned language features. In addition, the introduction of language targets into intervention roughly aligned with typical emergence of language features—typically developing children begin to use prepositions and coordinating conjunctions before using subordinating conjunctions (Justice & Ezell, 2002; Vasilyeva, Waterfall, & Huttenlocher, 2008).

On the script sheets, to the left of each script (textual line) was a small picture of Fran (½ × ½ inch), which we referred to as an icon. This icon was placed at the beginning of each of the five scripts on the script sheet that Fran was to read aloud. The icons served as nonspecific discriminative stimuli like the quotation marks in the Krantz and McClannahan (1993) study. The icons were placed on the script sheets in case Fran was unable to produce the trained targets and/or statements in the absence of all programmed stimuli. The icons proved useful in facilitating the transfer of stimulus control for the third and most difficult language target, subordinating conjunctions. After five intervention sessions in which Fran did not produce subordinating conjunctions in the assessment sessions, we created an additional script sheet with the textual scripts removed leaving only the five icons on the script sheet. This script sheet was generic because it only had the nonspecific discriminative stimuli (like quotation marks) on it; beside the five small icons, it was blank.

Teaching the scripts. Between baseline and intervention phases, instructors taught Fran to read each script. Individual scripts were attached to 3 × 5-inch note cards, and instructors used these to teach Fran to read each word of the text. All five scripts for each language target were taught simultaneously. After 2 days of reading the scripts approximately 16 times, the scripts were introduced in training sessions (i.e., intervention phase began for that language feature). Because we planned to *train loosely*, we did not require Fran to read each script perfectly before beginning the training sessions. This was important because we did not want her to memorize the scripts, which would have led to restricted stimulus control. After introducing the scripts into daily training sessions, Fran continued to practice reading the scripts at least once a day. However, when a new language feature entered into intervention, the previous set of five scripts (e.g., preposition scripts) was no longer used in training sessions or for additional practice. Fran only practiced the set of five scripts for the current language target (e.g., coordinating or subordinating conjunction scripts) on note cards and only the new set was presented on script sheets in training sessions. Even though the previous

Table 1. Scripts for Each Language Target

Language target	Target words	Scripts
Prepositions	In	1 script: I'm going to paint in this spot.
	On	2 scripts: The colors are pretty on the paper. It goes on the paper.
	With	2 scripts: I love to paint with this. Do you like to paint with me?
Coordinating conjunctions	And	3 scripts: I love to play and paint with you. I like painting and making beautiful pictures. Your picture is pretty and colorful.
	But	2 scripts: I paint on my paper but you paint on yours. Painting is fun, but messy.
Subordinating conjunctions	Because	2 scripts: I love to paint with you because you're fun. I like my picture because it's beautiful.
	When	3 scripts: Painting is fun, but messy when it gets on me. It's messy when I get it on my hands and fingers. Can I have that color when you're done?

targets' scripts were discarded and never reappeared, the later targets' scripts included earlier targets (see examples above and in Table 1).

Design

A multiple-baseline experimental design across three language features was employed for this study. Fran's conversational productions were assessed every day (Monday through Friday) across baseline and intervention conditions, which lasted approximately 9 weeks. Data for all three language targets were extracted from a single transcript of each assessment session. After four baseline sessions and three generalization probes, in which Fran did not use the selected targets more than once, we initiated training of scripts with prepositions. The second language feature trained was coordinating

conjunctions, and we introduced subordinating conjunctions last. Entrance of targets in intervention was based loosely on Fran's progress with previous targets and a time frame to ensure sufficient exposure to the current targets (about 2 weeks). More stringent decision rules were not used because Fran was exiting the university-based program at the end of the summer. All daily assessment sessions took place in her preschool program with training materials and with an instructor serving as the conversation partner.

To capture information regarding setting/stimulus generalization, we conducted a variety of generalization probes, which differed from the daily assessment sessions by at least one dimension (e.g., conversation partner, setting, materials). We systematically probed Fran's use of prepositions, coordinating conjunctions, and subordinating conjunctions in nontraining environments (home and kindergarten classroom), with nontraining materials (stamps and stamp pad), and with nontraining conversation partners (peers and mother) in baseline and following the 9-week intervention phase. In lieu of having typically developing peers available in Fran's preschool program, the investigators brought their children in to serve as confederate peers when possible. A maintenance probe was conducted following a 2-week summer break and after Fran's first 2 weeks in a general education kindergarten classroom (i.e., after a 4-week period of no intervention). The maintenance probe was conducted with the first author's 5-year-old son because he was in Fran's mainstream kindergarten class.

Procedures

Assessment sessions occurred each school-day morning (Monday through Friday) at approximately the same time. During the intervention phase, training sessions occurred about 15 min following each assessment session. The only difference between assessment and training sessions was that scripts and a prompter were present during the training sessions but not during the assessment sessions. Based on the work schedule established at the preschool, one of the three undergraduate instructors served as the conversation partner for the day and participated in assessment (except for generalization probes with Fran's peers and mother) and training sessions. The conversation partner sat across from Fran while painting with art supplies.

We arranged for transfer of stimulus control using *stimuli common* (i.e., art materials, familiar but rotating conversation partners, and a table) in assessment and training sessions. We selected four types of art supplies, with which Fran had limited exposure. Intervention materials included (a) Color Wonder finger paints with Color Wonder paper, (b) squeeze paints with art paper, and (c) dot paints with art paper. Flower and heart stamps, stamp pads, and art paper were used during probes for generalization to novel art materials. To maintain Fran's interest in the materials, none of these art supplies were available at any time other than during research sessions (i.e., assessment and training sessions). Prior to every assessment and training session, Fran selected which art supplies she wanted to use for that session from an array of three options (i.e., Color Wonder paints, squeeze paints, and dot paints). This daily preference assessment was important to prevent boredom or disliked materials from confounding Fran's motivation to talk during sessions. Researchers recorded Fran's choices to determine whether she repeatedly selected one type of art material. Fran independently varied her choice from day to day and session to session.

Assessment session procedures. Assessment sessions began when the conversation partner (i.e., instructor, mother, or peer) placed art supplies (in a rectangular container) on the table. At the same time, the partner started a digital voice recording device, which also tracked the length of the session. Fran and the conversation partner unpacked the materials and began painting. The conversation partner waited for Fran to begin the conversation. However, if Fran did not initiate the conversation within approximately 20 s of unpacking the materials, the conversation partner began talking about his/her own artwork. The conversation partner spoke naturally, modeled good talking, and replied to Fran's attempts to converse (*natural contingencies of reinforcement*). After 3 min, the conversation partner said, "It's time to clean up. Thanks for playing." Although textual scripts were never present during assessment sessions, the generic script sheet (i.e., sheet with five icons and no textual scripts) was included with the art materials for eight assessment sessions to facilitate transfer of stimulus control of subordinating conjunctions. Fran unpacked the script sheet and set it next to her on the table. No attention was drawn to it.

Training session procedures. Prior to training sessions, the first author, without looking, selected one of the three script sheets out of a folder to create a semi-random rotation of script sheets. The first author and a research assistant served as prompters, and one of them stood behind Fran during training sessions. Training sessions began when the conversation partner (i.e., instructor) placed the materials and script sheet (in a rectangular container) on the table. Fran unpacked the script sheet with the materials and placed it to the side of the table. If necessary, the prompter provided hand-over-hand guidance to help Fran take out the script sheet and place it near her but out of the way of her painting. To facilitate spontaneity of Fran's language, the conversation partner waited for Fran to initiate the conversation. If Fran did not begin speaking within approximately 20 s of unpacking the art supplies, the prompter manually guided her hand toward the script sheet by holding Fran's forearm and letting go as soon as Fran began pointing to the script. This was sufficient to prompt Fran to read the script and initiate the conversation. Using both of her hands on the sides of Fran's head, the prompter gently oriented Fran's head toward the conversation partner as needed. Once conversation began, the prompter waited for approximately 10 s of no talking before executing manual guidance to help Fran point to the next script line. After the first few training sessions, only a few manual prompts were required per training session. Twice during the training phase for subordinating conjunctions, the prompter provided a vocal prompt when Fran became frustrated because she was unable to read the script accurately. Otherwise, the prompter remained quiet during training sessions. The instructor spoke naturally, talking about his/her own artwork and replying to Fran's comments. When Fran had read all five scripts, the conversation partner said, "It's time to clean up. Thanks for playing." Training sessions lasted approximately 5 min, although the duration depended on how much Fran spoke in addition to the scripts.

Procedural fidelity. Prior to their involvement in the study, instructors and the research assistant who served as a prompter attended a training meeting consisting of a discussion of procedures, demonstration, and role-playing. Instructors were trained on five specific behaviors that were critical for being the conversation partner during assessment and training sessions: (a) place the art materials on the table without talking, (b) allow Fran to speak first or wait for 20 s (in assessment but not training sessions), (c) alternate speaking with Fran as in natural conversations, (d) respond to Fran's conversation statements enthusiastically but do not praise talking, and (e) when Fran is finished with her lines or 3 min had elapsed, say "Time to clean up. Thanks for playing."

For the training sessions, the prompters were trained on six steps: (a) stand behind Fran; (b) do not talk to Fran; (c) wait 20 s before prompting the start of the conversation; (d) after the conversation has begun, wait 10 s of no talking before prompting Fran to the next script; (e) use manual guidance holding Fran's forearm to help her point to the next script; and (f) if necessary, gently orient Fran's head toward the conversation partner. During the training of procedures, instructors and the prompter completed mock trials of assessment and training sessions while the first author recorded correct completion of steps using a fidelity checklist.

The same fidelity checklist was used to examine the extent to which assessment and training procedures were implemented as intended. With respect to assessment procedures, 32% of the sessions across all phases and conversation partners were observed for fidelity, and the average fidelity of implementation was 98% (80%–100%). With respect to training sessions, which included the conversation partner and the prompter, 31% of the sessions were observed for fidelity with an average fidelity of implementation of 99% (93%–100%).

Results

The frequency of target words emitted during 3-min assessment sessions for prepositions, coordinating conjunctions, and subordinating conjunctions is presented in Figure 1. During baseline sessions, Fran rarely used target language features during conversation about art. Once training began with prepositions, the frequency of use increased in a variably ascending pattern with a range of 0 to 4. Baseline levels of coordinating and subordinating conjunctions remained low when only prepositions were targeted during script and generalization training. When coordinating conjunctions were trained, Fran increasingly used coordinating conjunctions with a range from 0 to 4 and continued to use prepositions. Coordinating conjunctions followed a variable pattern with clear level changes. Subordinating conjunctions did not improve immediately following the introduction of training. After 5 days of training, Fran had not emitted a subordinating conjunction in an assessment session. We introduced the generic script sheet containing only the small pictures of Fran (i.e., nonspecific discriminative stimuli) into assessment sessions and conducted a probe with a different conversational partner (without the generic script sheet) after four sessions. Because no transfer was detected, the generic script sheet procedure was continued for another three sessions. This transfer of stimulus control strategy was sufficient to get Fran to use the subordinating conjunctions during assessment sessions. In the five generalization probes following the removal of the script sheet with icons, Fran continued to use subordinating conjunctions with a range from 0 to 4 when the script sheet was not present.

During baseline, Fran initiated conversation twice in the seven assessment sessions (29%), whereas during the intervention phase, Fran began the conversation in 86% of the sessions. Calculated percentages of untrained variations of the targeted language features were 81% for prepositions, 78% for coordinating conjunctions, and 16% for subordinating conjunctions.

Discussion

In this study, we sought to explore the feasibility of combining several generalization-enhancing strategies and script training procedures to affect the generalized use of complex language features of a child with autism. Results are interpreted to conclude that the integration of scripts and transfer of stimulus control procedures produced immediate improvements in prepositions and coordinating conjunctions and, with the brief addition of nonspecific discriminative stimuli, the effect was achieved for subordinating conjunctions. There are several reasons these results are significant. First, data were recorded during assessment sessions only, rather than assessing performance during training. Because textual scripts were never present during assessment sessions and the sessions reflected a natural context for talking, we essentially tested stimulus generalization every day. This intermittent exposure to the same conditions without the scripts could have served as a variation of script fading, as in the study by Woods and Poulson (2006).

In addition to our continuous measure of stimulus generalization, we also conducted situation generalization probes with typically developing peers and Fran's mother, in Fran's home and in her kindergarten classroom, and with art materials that were not used during training. After training, Fran used the targeted language features substantially more when probed for generalization than during baseline, and the improvements were maintained after 4 weeks of no training. Second, assessment sessions occurred daily before intervention sessions so the test for transfer to a nontraining context occurred 24 hr after training. Improvements detected following a significant delay from teaching are more robust than those that are recorded during training sessions. This is an important departure from most of the script training literature. Third, improvements in the use of prepositions and coordinating conjunctions were noticed after only one generalization training session. In previous research on script training with fading, several training sessions were necessary before equivalent improvements occurred.

In general, the degree of change observed may not appear to be substantial because the frequency of targets increased, at most, by four and results were variable. However, it is important to note that although we programmed five opportunities for the target language feature to occur during training sessions, opportunities for Fran to use prepositions, coordinating conjunctions, and subordinating conjunctions during assessment sessions were not programmed. Considering that Fran was free to emit any of the language targets and it took approximately 5 min for Fran to read all five of the scripts during training sessions, it would be unnatural for Fran to use any one of these target features more than 3 to 5 times during a 3-min conversation. Because we used frequency of targets rather than percentage of opportunities, we inspected the transcripts post hoc to determine how often Fran attempted to use a trained phrase but omitted the targeted language feature, constituting a failed opportunity. Interestingly, Fran seldom attempted a phrase in which the target features were unsuccessfully used. During baseline, Fran's language productions were simple phrases such as "You paint this one," "Purples gonna change," and "I make good grass." Instead of saying "The butterfly is orange and blue," Fran said, "The butterfly is orange. The butterfly is blue," avoiding the need to use a coordinating conjunction. In contrast, Fran said, "My flower is yellow *and* red" following training on coordinating conjunctions. In general, her language productions became more complex after training, suggesting a

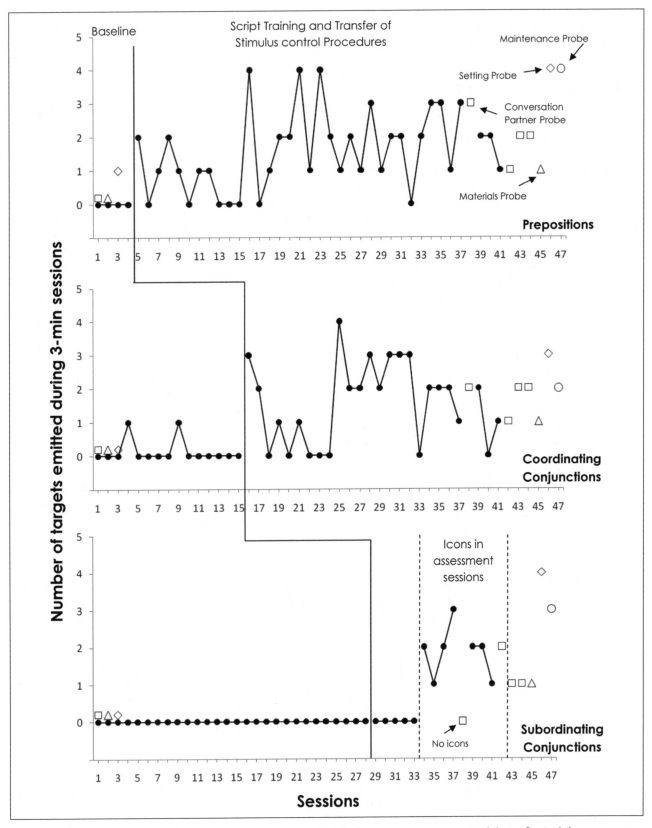

Figure 1. Number of prepositions, coordinating conjunctions, and subordinating conjunctions emitted during 3-min daily assessment sessions.

meaningful language improvement. For instance, during the follow-up session, Fran said, "You can paint a sky *on* your paper" and "I want to use that color *when* you're done."

As an estimate of spontaneity, we calculated the percentage of assessment sessions in which Fran started the conversation. Procedures allowed for a 20-s window from the time art materials were available to when the conversation partner started talking. If Fran started talking within this window, we considered the conversation initiated by her. In baseline, Fran began the conversation in less than a third of the sessions. She typically unpacked the art materials and started painting without acknowledging her conversation partner or attempting to gain his/her attention. Once training began, Fran was much more likely to begin the conversation; often, she started talking about the paints and telling her conversation partner what she was going to create as soon as the paint was available. The only methodological aspects of this study designed to increase conversation initiations were the instructor's delayed initiations during assessment sessions and prompting during training sessions for Fran to use the scripts to begin the conversation. Even though it is possible that these components of the training procedures contributed to increased initiations, the current study does not allow for definitive conclusions regarding an experimental effect.

To assess response generalization, we calculated the percentage of untrained uses for each of the targeted features. We intended to teach prepositions, coordinating conjunctions, and subordinating conjunctions as response classes using multiple exemplars (i.e., multiple targets within each class and multiple scripts for each target) and loose training of the scripts themselves (i.e., Fran was not required to be a proficient script reader before extending training to the conversation context). Because we introduced all five scripts at once, it slowed down her rate of decoding acquisition and prevented restricted stimulus control from developing. The effect of these strategies was evident when Fran struggled to remember the trained script word for word during assessment sessions. Occasionally, Fran said, speaking to herself, "That's not it. Try again." After a few attempts to say it as she learned it, she abandoned the attempt and changed it to suit the current situation, which we anticipated. Over time, untrained uses increased for all three language targets. In the final assessment sessions, few of the targets emitted were contained in trained phrases. The percentage of untrained uses was greatest for prepositions and lowest for subordinating conjunctions. This pattern was not unexpected for a number of reasons. First, Fran received more exposures to preposition scripts than coordinating conjunctions and more exposures to coordinating conjunctions than subordinating conjunctions. Second, a wider variety of scripts with prepositions were possible than with coordinating and subordinating conjunctions. Third, the amount of time between direct training and generalization probes was substantially larger for prepositions than for coordinating conjunctions, which was larger than for subordinating conjunctions. This interval could be responsible for some forgetting of the trained phrases and more forgetting occurs after larger intervals. Finally, the percentage of untrained responses followed the developmental sequence of the three language targets selected (Justice & Ezell, 2002; Vasilyeva et al., 2008). Prepositions and coordinating conjunctions were possibly emerging in her language repertoire, whereas subordinating conjunctions were not. Occasional baseline uses of prepositions and coordinating conjunctions support this notion. It is noteworthy that for Fran to produce a subordinating conjunction, the length of the sentence had to be longer than what she had ever produced in conversation.

One interesting finding of this study involves the temporary inclusion of the nonspecific discriminative stimuli (i.e., icons) in the assessment sessions. In the study by Krantz and McClannahan (1993), the quotation marks, which they were unable to eliminate, evoked a variety of conversational statements. Although this was a limitation in their study because it was unanticipated, the intentional use of nonspecific discriminative stimuli to promote spontaneity and generalization of language may have positive effects. We constructed our script sheets to include the visual icons in the pairing process. When transfer of language to assessment sessions did not occur for subordinating conjunctions, we elected to add the least interfering prompts possible and evaluate their effect before introducing the more intrusive textual scripts. The effect of this minimal prompting tactic was immediate. We believe that the icons enhanced the salience of the paired training and generalization stimuli and facilitated the transfer of stimulus control. Considering there is no one-to-one correspondence between a nonspecific discriminative stimulus and a specific response form, this strategy, if arranged thoughtfully, can help avoid restrictive stimulus control common during acquisition training. Although this conclusion is only speculative, the effect of this of type of strategy is worth exploring in future research.

Despite the importance of the findings, this study is limited in a number of ways. The most significant is that we investigated the effects of the combination of script training and transfer of stimulus control procedures with only one participant. Even though a multiple baseline across behaviors was used, notable effects were observed for only two of the three targets. Additional tactics were necessary for improvements to be shown with subordinating conjunctions. Thus, little can be concluded with respect to experimental effect of the intervention. Further replication with additional participants is needed.

Our procedures for training loosely (i.e., no specific performance criterion before beginning generalization training) and using natural contingencies of reinforcement (i.e., we did not prescribe what conversation partners should and should not say) add another limitation. It is possible that Fran's language productions were related in some way to the conversation partner's use of the target language features. Although no obvious connection was discovered through a review of the transcripts, this potential confound was not controlled for experimentally. We suggest other researchers examine methods for maximizing natural consequences and loose training while balancing the need for prescribed research procedures.

Conclusion

Developing a functional conversation repertoire requires acquisition of language and newly acquired language expressions be used with some spontaneity, that is, they be under the control of stimuli in the child's natural environment. Although these are necessary attributes, they are insufficient. It is also crucial that language be used in the variety of circumstances where it would be appropriate, even in circumstances different from those in which the training took place and with content different from that used in training. Moreover, language responses that are varied and flexible are more useful than those that are direct repeats of trained responses. Special attention to functional aspects of language such as spontaneity, stimulus/situation generalization, and response flexibility are necessary for teaching useful language to children with autism.

The exploratory nature of this study warrants further examination of the phenomena at play. It should be noted that because there were so many generalization-enhancing tactics used in this study, it is near impossible to speculate the influence of each. An important next step could be to evaluate the impact of each generalization-enhancing procedure independently, in a comparative fashion. It might be that they are more powerful in combination; however, that is currently unknown. Nonetheless, we were systematic in our logic for combing procedures, and therefore, the study may serve as a model for practitioners seeking maximum generalization when they are designing interventions for children with autism. Moreover, our study highlights areas where the literature is sparse. There are too few studies in which the strategies for transferring stimulus control are investigated as the primary independent variables. The majority of intervention research with children with autism addresses acquisition of behaviors, and the main generalization method used is train and hope (Stokes & Baer, 1977). The application of social communication interventions has certainly advanced beyond train and hope, yet such technology is rarely featured prominently in research.

In this study, we translated generalization technology into practical and implementable tactics. First, we used natural contingencies of reinforcement by allowing Fran to choose the activity for each session and ensuring that the conversation partner spoke naturally and enthusiastically in response to Fran's conversation statements. We expect that practitioners experience the greatest obstacles to training for generalization with children who are not easily motivated by social contingencies. However, if natural contingencies of reinforcement are essential to promote spontaneity and generalization of language, then improving the capacity of the natural consequences to function as reinforcers should be a priority. Our second tactic was to use multiple exemplars. The simultaneous introduction of several scripts containing the target language feature and the inclusion of previously learned targets in later scripts likely contributed to the response variation observed in use of prepositions and coordinating conjunctions. Fran was exposed to many different ways to use each target, which potentially contributed to her response flexibility. Training loosely was our third tactic, which can be seen in several procedures. The most obvious is that we did not require a mastery criterion for reading performance before introducing the generalization strategies. Other strategies, however, were the intentional loose conversation allowed from the partners, the daily exposure to the nontraining conditions of the assessment sessions, and exposure to several scripts at once reducing Fran's accuracy of script reading. Finally, we programmed for common stimuli in treatment and assessment sessions. These stimuli were taken directly from a context that we anticipated would be natural for Fran in the near future (e.g., table, art materials, conversation partner). Although we would have preferred to train using typically developing peers because they are more natural conversation partners than instructors, they were unavailable in her preschool program. Instead of programming using typically developing peers, we were able to test whether our other strategies were sufficient to produce generalization to nontraining conversation partners.

Although these strategies were successful in Fran's situation, we strongly encourage additional researchers to verify these effects using stronger controls and more participants. These findings and the logical conceptualization of relevant independent variables may assist researchers and practitioners in effecting significant generalized behavior change. Nonetheless, a logical analysis should not supplant an experimental analysis.

Acknowledgment

The first author would like to express gratitude to the research assistants, students, and administration of the Autism Support Services: Education, Research and Training (ASSERT) program for their commitment to excellence through research.

Declaration of Conflicting Interests

The author(s) declared no potential conflicts of interest with respect to the research, authorship, and/or publication of this article.

Funding

The author(s) received no financial support for the research and/or publication of this article.

References

American Psychiatric Association. (2000). *Diagnostic and statistical manual of mental disorders* (4th ed., text rev.). Washington, DC: Author.

Argott, P., Townsend, D. B., Sturmey, P., & Poulson, C. L. (2008). Increasing the use of empathic statements in the presence of a non-verbal affective stimulus in adolescents with autism. *Research in Autism Spectrum Disorders, 2*, 341–352.

Brown, J. L., Krantz, P. J., McClannahan, L. E., & Poulson, C. L. (2008). Using script fading to promote natural environment stimulus control of verbal interactions among youth with autism. *Research in Autism Spectrum Disorders, 2*, 480–497.

Carr, E. G. (1982). Sign language. In R. L. Koegel, A. Rincover, & A. L. Egel (Eds.), *Educating and understanding autistic children* (pp. 142–157). San Diego, CA: College-Hill Press.

Carr, E. G., & Kologinsky, D. (1983). Acquisition of sign language by autistic children. II: Spontaneity and generalization effects. *Journal of Applied Behavior Analysis, 16*, 297–314.

Carter, M., & Hotchkis, G. D. (2002). A conceptual analysis of communicative spontaneity. *Journal of Intellectual & Developmental Disabilities, 27*, 168–190.

Charlop, M. H., Schreibman, L., & Thibodeau, M. G. (1985). Increasing spontaneous verbal responding in autistic children using a time delay procedure. *Journal of Applied Behavior Analysis, 18*, 155–166.

Chiang, H., & Carter, M. (2008). Spontaneity of communication in individuals with autism. *Journal of Autism and Developmental Disorders, 38*, 693–705.

Cooper, J. O., Heron, T. E., & Heward, W. L. (Eds.). (2007). *Applied behavior analysis* (2nd ed.). Upper Saddle River, NJ: Pearson Education.

Halle, J. W. (1987). Teaching language in the natural environment: An analysis of spontaneity. *Journal of the Association for Persons With Severe Handicaps, 12*, 28–37.

Justice, L. M., & Ezell, H. K. (2002). *The syntax handbook: Everything you learned about syntax (but forgot)*. Eau Claire, WI: Thinking Publications.

Koegel, L. K. (2000). Interventions to facilitate communication in autism. *Journal of Autism and Developmental Disorders, 30*, 383–391.

Krantz, P. J., & McClannahan, L. E. (1993). Teaching children with autism to initiate to peers: Effects of a script-fading procedure. *Journal of Applied Behavior Analysis, 26*, 121–132.

McClannahan, L. E., & Krantz, P. J. (2005). *Teaching conversation to children with autism: Scripts and script fading*. Bethesda, MD: Woodbine House.

McConnell, S. R. (2002). Interventions to facilitate social interaction for young children with autism: Review of available research and recommendations for educational intervention and future research. *Journal of Autism and Developmental Disorders, 32*, 351–372.

Newman, T. M., Macomber, D., Naples, A. J., Babitz, T., Vokmar, F., & Grigorenko, E. L. (2007). Hyperlexia in children with autism spectrum disorders. *Journal of Autism and Developmental Disorders, 37*, 760–774.

Quill, K. (1997). Instructional considerations for young children with autism: The rationale for visually cued instruction. *Journal of Autism and Developmental Disorders, 27*, 697–714.

Robertson, S. A. (2007). Assessment of preschool and early school-age children with developmental language disorders. In A. G. Kamhi, J. J. Masterson, & K. Apel (Eds.), *Clinical decision making in developmental language disorders* (pp. 39–54). Baltimore, MD: Paul H. Brooks.

Sigafoos, J., & Reichle, J. (1993). Establishing spontaneous verbal behavior. In R. A. Gable & S. F. Warren (Eds.), *Strategies for teaching students with mild to severe mental retardation* (pp. 191–230). Baltimore, MD: Paul H. Brookes.

Stokes, T. F., & Baer, D. (1977). An implicit technology of generalization. *Journal of Applied Behavior Analysis, 10*, 349–367.

Vasilyeva, M., Waterfall, H., & Huttenlocher, J. (2008). Emergence of syntax: Commonalities and differences across children. *Developmental Science, 11*, 84–97.

Woods, J. M., & Poulson, C. L. (2006). The use of scripts to increase the verbal initiations of children with developmental disabilities to typically developing peers. *Education & Treatment of Children, 29*, 437–457.

H HAMMILL INSTITUTE
I ON DISABILITIES

Focus on Autism and Other
Developmental Disabilities
27(4) 237–246
© 2012 Hammill Institute on Disabilities
Reprints and permission:
sagepub.com/journalsPermissions.nav
DOI: 10.1177/1088357612457986
http://foa.sagepub.com

Effect of Observing-Response Procedures on Overselectivity in Individuals With Autism Spectrum Disorders

Phil Reed, DPhil[1], Laura Altweck, BSc[1], Laura Broomfield, PhD[1],
Anna Simpson, MSc[1], and Louise McHugh, PhD[2]

Abstract

Stimulus overselectivity occurs when one aspect of the environment controls behavior at the expense of other equally salient aspects. Stimulus overselectivity can be reduced for some individuals with learning disabilities, if they engage in an observing response in which they point to, touch, or name each of the stimuli prior to selecting the one requested. To see whether this would apply to another population, a total of 55 participants with autism spectrum disorders (ASD) were trained on match-to-sample (MTS), or simple discrimination tasks, to determine whether overselectivity could be eliminated by using an observing response. MTS tasks were presented in a table-top format as well as on a computer. The observing-response procedure did not eliminate overselectivity for any of the participants, regardless of age, task, or format of presentation. These results are interpreted to call to question the effectiveness of this procedure in this context for individuals with ASD.

Keywords

autism spectrum disorders, stimulus overselectivity, observing response

Stimulus overselectivity is the term used to describe the phenomenon whereby one aspect of the environment comes to control behavior at the expense of other equally salient aspects of the environment. Overselectivity has a high level of occurrence in those with autism spectrum disorders (ASD; Lovaas & Schreibman, 1971), although it is not restricted to this population (Dube & McIlvane, 1999; McHugh & Reed, 2007). In terms of the clinical implications of overselectivity, responding that is restricted to a small set of cues can severely inhibit the individual's ability to learn about complex objects (Reynolds, Newsom, & Lovaas, 1974; Varni, Lovaas, Kogel, & Everett, 1979), can diminish the impact of teaching interventions (Broomfield, McHugh, & Reed, 2007), and can cause severe difficulties for social interaction (Birnie-Selwyn & Guerin, 1997; Cook, Anderson, & Rincover, 1982).

The use of an observing-response procedure has been considered by several investigators to combat overselectivity (Broomfield et al., 2007; Constantine & Sidman, 1975; Stromer, McIlvane, Dube, & Mackay, 1993). An observing response requires the individual first to attend to each individual stimulus (by touching, pointing, and/or naming) before the instructor requests an action (e.g., give me cup).

This promotes exposure to a discriminative stimulus and brings sensory receptors into contact with the environmental stimuli (Wyckoff, 1952). Ensuring that all aspects of the stimulus initially are sampled should, in principle, overcome any potential attention deficits experienced by the participants because not all aspects of the stimuli are initially perceived (Dube & McIlvane, 1999).

Constantine and Sidman (1975) examined a delayed match-to-sample task (MTS) with picture stimuli as the sample and comparison stimuli, with four participants with learning disabilities. When the sample picture was available at the same time as the comparison, the participants performed accurately. However, performance was poor in the delayed condition (i.e., when the sample was removed prior to the presentation of the comparison). In contrast, when names, rather than pictures, were presented as samples,

[1]Swansea University, UK
[2]University College Dublin, Ireland

Corresponding Author:
Phil Reed, Department of Psychology, Swansea University, Singleton Park, Swansea SA2 8PP, UK
Email: p.reed@swansea.ac.uk

three out of the four participants matched pictures to the names, even under the delayed condition.

Constantine and Sidman (1975) suggested that the use of a naming-observing procedure increased accuracy scores in MTS tasks and supported the use of observing-response procedures to aid learning in individuals with learning disabilities. Of course, not all individuals with learning disabilities have naming abilities, so the study of nonverbal observing-response procedures (e.g., pointing) may offer greater generality of the results.

Dube and McIlvane (1999) compared accuracy in a delayed-MTS condition with accuracy when an observing-response procedure (without naming) was adopted. This procedure meant that the participants with learning disabilities made simultaneous identity-matching responses that required observation and discrimination of both samples. When an observing-response intervention was introduced, the accuracy scores improved relative to when the observing response was not used. However, it should be noted that accuracy scores returned to baseline when the observing response was no longer used. A similar effect was noted by Broomfield et al. (2007), who demonstrated that an observing-response procedure had only a limited usefulness in a typically developing population of adults who were exposed to a concurrent task (a procedure known to induce overselective responding in healthy adults; Reed & Gibson, 2005); the effects of an observing-response procedure in eliminating overselectivity disappeared when it was withdrawn, leaving no lasting benefit to the participants.

Thus, although there is evidence that an observing-response procedure can reduce overselectivity (Constantine & Sidman, 1975; Stromer et al., 1993), this procedure may not promote long-term effects (Broomfield et al., 2007; Dube & McIlvane, 1999). Rather, the procedural benefits of an observing-response intervention appear to be confined to the period of application of the intervention. This finding is a drawback to any potential treatment based on observing-response interventions, and certainly requires further study.

In the current studies, we sought to ascertain the effectiveness of the observing-response procedure for the elimination of overselectivity in a sample of individuals with ASD. Although this procedure has been used extensively as an intervention for overselectivity in populations with learning disabilities (Constantine & Sidman, 1975; Dube & McIlvane, 1999), there are no demonstrations of the use of an observing-response procedure to elevate overselectivity in a population with ASD.

In tackling this issue, it should be noted that there are multiple possible procedures that could be used in terms of observing responses (e.g., pointing and/or naming) and multiple training contexts in which they could be used (e.g., MTS, simple discriminations). Given this consideration, we used a variety of different techniques: table top MTS with pointing (Experiment 1), automated MTS with pointing (Experiment 2), and simple discrimination training with pointing and naming (Experiment 3). Although this makes the individual studies somewhat different from one another, they all address the same basic issue of whether observing responses facilitate learning in children with ASD.

General Method

Common Procedures

The recruiting and assessment procedures were the same across all three experiments. Participants for each study were recruited by asking the parents of the children to volunteer their children's time. All of the participants were diagnosed with autistic disorder or pervasive developmental disorder–not otherwise specified and had no other diagnoses. The diagnoses were made by a specialist pediatrician, not affiliated with the research, on the basis of criteria from the *Diagnostic and Statistical Manual of Mental Disorders* and clinical judgment. All the participants also had a statement of special educational needs from their local education authority that included autism, and they all attended a special school for students with ASD.

The participants' diagnoses were supported by the administration of the Autism Behavior Checklist (ABC; Krug, Arick, & Almond, 1980). This was completed by the parents of the children to assess the severity of the autism of each child and was returned with the consent form. The ABC is a 57-item checklist, grouped into five areas: sensory, relating, body and object use, language, and social and self-help skills. A total score of 67 or more is taken by Krug et al. (1980) to suggest probable autism. Scores between 55 and 67 suggest possible autism. Reports on reliability have been high (Volkmar et al., 1988), although the convergence among the ABC and other instruments has not been good. This possibly reflects the ABC's somewhat broad-based symptom focus (Shaffer, Lucas, & Richters, 1999). Thus, it is important to note that the measure may not give a similar picture of the child's autism as other instruments; however, the ABC was still considered useful in the present context because (a) no special training in administration or scoring is required, and, in the current study, it was to be completed by parents, who tend, on average, to produce higher scores than teachers (Volkmar et al., 1988) and (b) it was to be used as a research tool gauging the relative effects of autistic symptomatology across the participants, rather than to make absolute judgments regarding the impact of symptoms.

Once parental consent had been obtained, along with the parent-rated ABC questionnaire, each experiment was conducted in a quiet room in the participants' schools. The participants sat besides the experimenter, and a teaching

Table 1. Participant Characteristics Across Studies

Experiment	n	Male:Female	Age (years)			ABC			BPVS (years)		
			M	Range	SD	M	Range	SD	M	Range	SD
1	15	13:2	12.6	7.5–17.2	2.8	69.9	56–89	9.4	4.2	2.3–8.4	1.7
2	22	19:3	12.6	7.8–17.1	2.9	69.2	57–89	8.2	9.2	4.8–14.4	3.3
3	18	17:1	12.3	7.6–17.1	3.3	68.8	56–85	7.6	3.9	2.0–8.1	1.9

Note: ABC = Autism Behavior Checklist (Krug, Arick, & Almond, 1980); BPVS = *British Picture Vocabulary Scale* (Dunn, Dunn, Whetton, & Pintile, 1982).

assistant (different for each child) sat behind them. The presence of the teaching assistant was to make the child feel more comfortable/familiar with the testing situation and to act as an independent rater of the behaviors (in all cases, the scores from the experimenter and teaching assistant were identical). Initially, the participants were administered the *British Picture Vocabulary Scale* (BPVS; Dunn, Dunn, Whetton, & Pintile, 1982) by the experimenter conducting the study, according to the manual, to ascertain their verbal mental age according to their receptive language capacity. The BPVS does not require any speaking, writing, or reading; the child simply points to picture cards. This means that this test is suitable for use with children with special needs. The child is asked to point to one picture that matches a spoken word out of a choice of four pictures. This test is standardized for use on children in the United Kingdom between 3 and 17 years of age. It has an internal reliability of .93 and, according to Dunn et al. (1982), correlates .59 with the *Comprehension Scale* of the *Reynell Developmental Language Scales*. The BPVS took approximately 20 min to administer. Participant characteristics for each of the three experiments are provided in Table 1.

For each experiment, participants were randomly assigned to one of two groups: an experimental group or a control group. Randomization was accomplished by tossing a coin to determine group membership.

Experiment 1

Experiment 1 explored the effectiveness of an observing-response procedure to reduce overselectivity in 15 participants with ASD. Broomfield et al. (2007) and Dube and McIlvane (1999) found that an observing-response procedure reduced overselectivity in individuals with learning disabilities, but it is not certain that this procedure would be effective for individuals with ASD. In addition, Broomfield et al. and Dube and McIlvane discovered that the beneficial effects did not last post-intervention. Thus, a further aim of the present experiment was to investigate whether an observing-response procedure would reduce overselectivity in participants with ASD once it was withdrawn.

Figure 1. Examples of stimulus components symbols.

Method

Participants. Nineteen participants were initially tested for the first experiment. Two participants did not complete the first experimental phase of the study, and two participants could not complete the BPVS, so these four participants were excluded from the experiment. Table 1 contains information about the participants who completed the study. The mean age, ABC, and BPVS for the experimental group ($n = 8$) were 12.6 years, 69.8, and 4.1 years. The mean age, ABC, and BPVS for the control group ($n = 7$) were 12 years, 70.1, and 4.7 years. No group differences on these variables were statistically significant, all $ts < 1$. One female was in each group.

MTS Stimuli. The stimuli components used in the MTS task were symbols obtained from various fonts in Microsoft Word 2000. These fonts were Wingdings, Windings 2, and Symbol (see Figure 1 for examples).

There were three elements in each sample compound, and there were three samples used (i.e., ABC, DEF, GHI). In the comparison stimuli, there were three elements, one of which was previously presented in the sample stimulus and the other two elements came from the other samples (e.g., AEH). The three elements of the sample and comparison stimuli were presented on A4 sheets of paper. The specific stimuli used as ABC and so forth were different for each participant to avoid any stimulus-specific effects.

Procedure. The experiment was conducted in two phases: Phase 1, in which the experimental group of participants received MTS training with an observing-response procedure and a control group received MTS training with no observing response, and Phase 2, in which both groups received MTS training with no observing response.

Phase 1. All participants performed an MTS task. The participants were told,

> You will be shown a piece of paper with three symbols on it, please try to remember the symbols. You will then be shown another piece of paper with three symbols on. One of the symbols will be the same as on the piece of paper you saw before. Please point to the symbol you think you saw on the previous piece of paper.

Nine symbols were presented in three, three-element compound stimuli (e.g., ABC, DEF, GHI) during this training phase. Participants were shown an A4 sheet displaying one of the sets of three stimuli for 5 s as the sample. Participants were then shown (as the comparison) one of the sample stimuli, along with two of the other stimuli. For example, if ABC was shown as a sample, either A, B, or C would then be shown with two other elements (one from each of the other three-element compounds, such as DG or EH) in the comparison stimulus. Each participant received all combinations of the elements as comparisons (with all comparison stimuli being presented in left-to-right order, ADG, GAD, DGA, etc.), meaning that there were 54 comparison-sample trials in total (18 for each three-element sample).

Participants needed to select the symbol that was the same as the one on the previous compound. The experimenter told participants whether their choice was correct or incorrect.

For the control group, these were the only contingencies in operation. For the experimental group, the participants performed the MTS task with an observing response. These participants were asked to point to all three symbols on the sample card, one by one, to ensure that they acknowledged their presence.

Participants in the experimental group were told,

> You will be shown a piece of paper with three symbols on it. Please point to the symbol on the left . . . [once they pointed to that symbol] . . . Please point to the symbol in the middle . . . [once they pointed to that symbol] . . . Please point to the symbol on the right . . . [once they pointed to that symbol].

Naming was not used as an observing response because of the limited verbal ability of some of the children. Once this was performed, the MTS trial commenced.

Phase 2. After a period of 20 min following the completion of Phase 1, during which the participants rested and were not in the experimental room, a new set of stimuli was presented to participants in a MTS task. The new stimuli

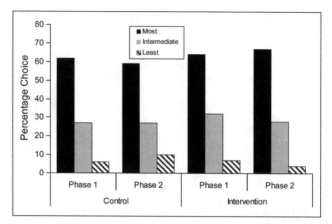

Figure 2. Mean percentage of the most, intermediate, and least chosen stimulus elements across the two groups in both phases of Experiment 1.

consisted of nine stimuli from the same fonts as described for Phase 1, but different from those employed in Phase 1, and were presented in 54 trials, in the same manner and procedure as in the first phase, except that experimental group no longer had the observing-response procedure in place.

Results and Discussion

For each participant, the mean percentage times that the most, intermediate, and least chosen stimulus elements were correctly chosen were calculated. This was achieved by determining how many times each element had been correctly chosen when it was presented in the comparison (i.e., how many times out of 18), and this was converted into a percentage. The elements were then ordered into most to least chosen for each participant. The most, intermediate, and least chosen symbols were not the same for each participant, suggesting no inherent preference for particular stimuli. The percentage times that each stimulus was chosen is displayed in Figure 2.

Inspection of Figure 2 shows a clear difference among percentages of times that the most, intermediate, and least were chosen. However, there was little difference between the two groups and little difference across the two phases. A three-factor, mixed-model analysis of variance (ANOVA), with group (experimental and control) as a between-participant factor, and phase (Phases 1 and 2) and stimulus (most, intermediate, and least), was conducted on these data, and revealed only a statistically significant main effect of stimulus, $F(2, 26) = 131.22$, $p < .001$. These results suggest that the children displayed overselectivity, but that the effect of an observing response without naming was negligible.

Figure 3 displays the group-mean difference in percentage times that the most and intermediate, and most

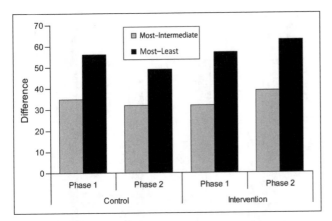

Figure 3. Difference between most and intermediately chosen, and the most and least chosen, stimuli in each phase for both groups during Experiment 1.

and least, chosen stimuli were picked. Inspection of these data shows little impact of the observing-response procedure in Phase 1 for the experimental group relative to the control group. A mixed-model ANOVA (Group × Phase × Stimulus) was conducted on these data and revealed a statistically significant main effect of difference, $F(1, 13) = 314.07$, $p < .001$, but no other main effects or interactions were statistically significant, all ps > .10.

These data are interpreted to confirm that large overselectivity effects emerge with children with ASD, but that there was no effect of an observing response on this effect in these participants. This finding stands in contrast to several other demonstrations of the effectiveness of an observing response with other populations (Broomfield et al., 2007; Constantine & Sidman, 1975; Dube & McIlvane, 1999). Phase 2 was intended to determine whether any effect of the observing response on MTS performance could be maintained and generalized, but because there was no impact of the observing-response procedure, it is not surprising that there was no difference in the groups' performances in Phase 2. Prior to the discussion of the implications of this finding, it was thought prudent to explore this null effect in other procedures to confirm its generality.

Experiment 2

In Experiment 2, our aim was to extend the research by using an automated MTS, rather than "table top," procedure, in an attempt to further explore the effectiveness of an observing-response procedure to reduce overselectivity in individuals with ASD. If similar null results were obtained using a different form of MTS procedure, then more weight could be placed on the lack of an observing-response effect on reducing overselectivity.

Method

Participants. Table 1 contains information about the participants who completed Experiment 2. The mean age, ABC, and BPVS for the experimental group ($n = 11$) were 12.3 years, 70.2, and 8.9 years. The mean age, ABC, and BPVS for the control group ($n = 11$) were 12.9 years, 67.7, and 9.1 years. No group differences on these variables were statistically significant, all ts < 1. One female was in the experimental group, and 2 females were in the control group. None of the participants in Experiment 1 were included in Experiment 2.

MTS Stimuli. The stimuli to be used in the automated MTS procedure were drawn from the same set as employed in Experiment 1. The experiment was conducted on a Fujitsu Siemens laptop computer with a 150 GHZ processor.

Procedure. The participants sat in front of the computer and instructions appeared on the screen, explaining that this was a MTS procedure:

> This is a match-to-samples task. Three symbols will appear in the middle of the screen for 5 s, please study these symbols. Four symbols will then appear in the corners of the screen. Two of the four symbols will be the same as the symbols seen on the previously shown screen. Please select one of the symbols that you believe matches the previous symbols using the mouse. There will be a practice session to begin with.

The experimenter read these instructions to the participants. The instructions were then explained, "There will be three pictures, then four pictures. You must try to choose one you have seen before."

There were 10 practice trials; the first trial was demonstrated by the experimenter, so that the participants could see what they were meant to do. The stimuli A, B, and C were presented, followed by two of the target stimuli (AB, AC, or BC) and two novel stimuli (DE, EF, or DF). The four stimuli appeared in the corners of the screen. Participants had to click on one of the stimulus elements that they thought they had previously seen. The participants were given feedback of "very good" with a picture of a cartoon dog dancing, if they chose one of the correct stimulus elements (i.e., a stimulus element that appeared in the sample). They were given feedback of "oops," with cartoon of a bear looking sad, if they chose the wrong stimulus element (i.e., a stimulus element that had not appeared in the sample). The stimuli were presented an equal number of times, so AB, BC, and AC were each presented 3 times, and each element A, B, and C was presented 6 times. The participants completed the remaining 9 practice trials by themselves.

Participants completed the practice trials in an average of 3 min. Once the participants had completed the 10 practice trials, they were informed that the experiment was to begin.

Phase 1. The procedure was as outlined above. The participants in the observing conditions also were informed that they needed to click on each of the three stimuli that appeared on screen, and a red dot would appear underneath to indicate that they had done so. There were nine trials presenting the sample and comparison stimuli.

Phase 2. This was the interval before the retesting phase, and the participants were given the following instructions: "Two symbols will appear on screen. Use the mouse to select one. You will be given feedback of correct or incorrect for your choices." Again, the experimenter explained to the children what they had to do. The side on which the "correct" novel stimulus appeared (left or right) was alternated across trials. Participants were given feedback of "very good," when they selected the one stimulus by clicking on it with the mouse. They were given feedback of "oops" if they selected the other stimulus. This continued until the participant got 10 correct answers consecutively. Which stimulus was correct was arbitrary. This phase of the experiment provided an interval between Phases 1 and 3 of the experiment. This phase was inserted to provide a break between the initial testing (Phase 1) and the determination if any improvement due to the observing response was maintained (Phase 3), and on average took about 5 min to complete.

Phase 3. This phase was the same as Phase 1; however, no corrective feedback was given, and there were no practice trials. Both conditions were the same as one another, so no observing response was used for the participants in the observing condition.

Results and Discussion

From the sample comparison selections, the percentage of times the most, intermediate, and least chosen stimulus elements were chosen was calculated for each participant. The most, intermediate, and least chosen stimuli were not the same for each participant, suggesting that there were no consistent inherent preferences for the stimuli. Figure 4 displays the mean percentage selections for the most, intermediate, and least chosen stimuli in the observing and control conditions for the test and the retest phases.

It can be seen from Figure 4 that there was only a very slight alteration in differentiation among the most, intermediate, and least chosen stimuli in the observing condition, in comparison with the control condition in Phase 1. However, it is clear from these data that the observing response did not have a particularly dramatic effect on reducing the degree of overselectivity relative to the control group. That there was little impact of the observing-response procedure when it was implemented in Phase 1 makes it unsurprising that

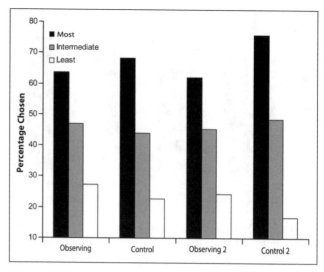

Figure 4. Mean accuracy scores for the most, intermediate, and least chosen element of the compound in each of the conditions in Experiment 2.

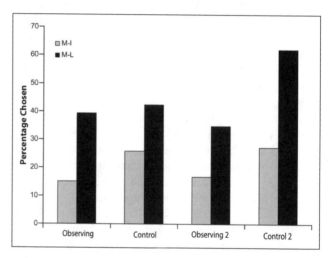

Figure 5. Mean difference between the most accurately chosen stimulus and the stimulus chosen with intermediate accuracy, and the most accurately chosen stimulus and the least accurately chosen stimulus, in Experiment 2.
Note: M-I = most–intermediate; M-L = most–least.

there was little change in the performance of the groups in Phase 3. A three-factor, mixed-model ANOVA (Stimulus Type × Phase × Group) revealed that there was a statistically significant main effect of stimulus type, $F(2, 40) = 94.01$, $p < .0001$, but none of the other main effects, nor interactions, were statistically significant, $ps > .05$.

The difference between the most and intermediate, and between the most and least, chosen stimuli was calculated for each participant. Figure 5 shows the mean differences across the participants in the observing and control conditions for the test and retest phases; the larger the difference in this score, the greater the degree of overselectivity displayed.

The data in Figure 5 are interpreted to reveal an effect of the observing response somewhat more clearly than the data described above, although the effect is, again, slight. It can be seen from inspection of the data from Phase 1 that there was numerically slightly less overselectivity in the experimental condition than the control condition, but only for the most to intermediate comparison. In fact, this effect is seen to a greater extent in Phase 3 This does not necessarily suggest that the observing response is maintaining, as the change responsible for the effect in Phase 3 is the overselectivity increasing in the control group, for which there is no clear explanation.

A mixed-model ANOVA (Group × Stimulus × Phase) conducted on these data showed that there was a statistically significant main effect of stimulus type, $F(2, 40) = 33.71$, $p < .0001$, there was a statistically significant main effect of group, $F(1, 20) = 6.43$, $p < .05$, and a statistically significant interaction among the three factors, $F(1, 20) = 4.71$, $p < .05$; none of the other main effects, nor interactions, were statistically significant, $ps > .05$. To further analyze these data, separate mixed-model ANOVAs (Stimulus type × Group) were performed on each phase. This analysis of Phase 1 showed stimulus type to be statistically significant, $F(1, 20) = 13.60$, $p < .001$, but neither the main effect of group nor the interaction between the two factors was statistically significant, $Fs < 1$. The mixed-model ANOVA for Phase 3 showed that there were statistically significant main effects of stimulus type, $F(1, 10) = 40.02$, $p < .0001$, and group, $F(1, 10) = 9.56$, $p < .01$, but there was no statistically significant interaction between the two, $F(1, 10) = 3.96$, $p > .05$. Simple effects analyses showed that there were no statistically significant differences between the groups for the most and intermediate scores in Phase 1, nor in Phase 3, $ps > .05$. There was no statistically significant difference between the most and least chosen scores between the groups in Phase 1, $F < 1$, but there was a statistically significant difference between the most and least scores in Phase 3, $F(1, 20) = 8.83$, $p < .05$.

From the results, it can be seen that overselectivity was observed in this population using an automated procedure. This suggests that overselectivity is observed in a population with ASD using a MTS task, and this effect can be seen in an automated procedure as well as in the table-top procedures used in Experiment 1. However, the results with respect to the effect of the observing response were not strong, replicating the lack of a clear effect reported in Experiment 1. There was more overselectivity in the control group in comparison with the experimental group. However, this was only seen in the retest phase. Scores in the observing condition did not differ between the test and retest phases. Thus, although the current experiment corroborated the existence of overselectivity in the clinical group using

this procedure, it could find no evidence to support the effectiveness of the observing response as an intervention to ameliorate this effect. This may not be entirely surprising given the lack of existing literature with respect to ASD.

Experiment 3

Observing-response procedures have been found to reduce overselectivity in participants with learning disabilities (Constantine & Sidman, 1975; Dube & McIlvane, 1999; Stromer et al., 1993) but were not noted for the participants with ASD in Experiments 1 and 2. Given this finding, it is questionable how useful this procedure is for remediating the overselectivity problem in this population. The current experiment aimed to explore whether any reduction in overselectivity would occur in a sample with ASD when the observing response was in place in a simple learning discrimination task, which has been used a number of times to investigate this phenomena in this population (Reed, Broomfield, McHugh, McCausland, & Leader, 2008). If an observing-response procedure was successful, then children in the observing group would display less overselectivity than the children in the control group. If the intervention was not successful in reducing overselectivity with a second procedure (simple discrimination as opposed to MTS), it would add to the suggestion that, at least for overselectivity with this population, an observing-response procedure may not be the intervention of choice.

Method

Participants. Twenty children with ASD were initially recruited, but two of the children did not meet the training criteria because they failed to complete the task. Table 1 contains information about the participants who completed the study. The mean age, ABC, and BPVS for the experimental group ($n = 10$) were 12.4 years, 67.7, and 4.1 years. The mean age, ABC, and BPVS for the control group ($n = 8$) were 12.4 years, 69.6, and 4.0 years. No group differences on these variables were statistically significant, all $ts < 1$. One female was in the experimental group, but there were no females in the control group. None of the participants in Experiment 3 were included in Experiment 1 or 2.

Discrimination stimuli. Stimulus cards used in this experiment, measuring 15 cm × 10 cm, were the same as those described by Reed et al. (2008). Each card displayed pictures of two items to form a compound stimulus. The elements employed in the experiment were a hand, a cup and saucer, a bed, and a butterfly. The elements that were combined to produce the compounds were different for each individual (e.g., hand and bed for one participant, hand and butterfly for another participant, bed and hand for a third participant).

Procedure. The cards depicting the compound stimuli were placed in the center of the table between the participant and the experimenter. Participants were presented with two white cards simultaneously. Each card contained two stimulus elements (e.g., they were presented with an AB+ CD− discrimination task). Participants were rewarded for pointing at, say, the "hand and teacup" (i.e., AB+) rather than the "bed and butterfly" (e.g., CD−). The combination of stimulus elements on the reinforced card was different for each participant to avoid the potential confound of some stimuli being intrinsically more salient than others. Thus, on any given trial, participants were presented with one compound stimulus (e.g., "AB"), which, if pointed at, resulted in positive feedback in the form of the experimenter saying "yes," and another card ("CD") that received negative feedback (i.e., the experimenter saying "no"). The positions of the cards were randomized; 50% of the time the correct card (AB) was presented on the left and 50% of the time on the right. Participants were said to have acquired the discrimination once they had responded correctly 10 times.

The children in the observing condition had to name the stimuli on the cards and then point to a card, as described above. A naming-observing response was adopted in this study at the request of the school. Some of the children did not understand the instruction pointing. For these children, the experimenter held out his or her hand, and the child placed the chosen card into the experimenter's hand. If the child chose the "wrong" card, the experimenter would close his hand and avoid eye contact. This took an average of 5 min.

Children in the control group performed the discrimination training identically to that described above but without having to name the stimuli. It took an average of 6 min for the participants in the control group to achieve mastery.

Results and Discussion

The control participants on average took 28.67 (±14.45) trials during training to choose the correct card 10 times consecutively, whereas the experimental group took 21.56 (±11.53) trials to reach criterion. There was no significant difference between the groups in terms of trials to mastery, $t(16) = 1.15, p > .05$.

Figure 6 shows the mean percentage of times that each of the stimuli (most and least) was selected for both groups. Inspection of Figure 6 shows that there was overselectivity in both groups, which, while slightly less for the experimental group, was due to less learning about the overselected stimulus than in the control group (which would not be expected if the observing response was aiding performance). There was little difference between the levels of selection of the underselected stimulus in each group. A mixed-model ANOVA (Group × Stimulus type) revealed that there was a statistically significant main effect of stimulus type,

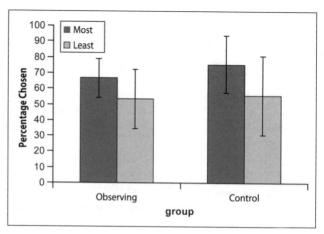

Figure 6. Mean percentage chosen for the most and least selected stimulus in each group during Experiment 3.

$F(1, 16) = 19.05, p < .0001$, but there was no statistically significant effect of group, $F < 1$, or interaction, $F < 1$.

These results are interpreted to conclude that participants in the observing condition showed significant degrees of overselectivity, even when the observing response was in place. This failure to show reduction in overselectivity in participants with ASD using a simple discrimination procedure replicates the failure noted in Experiments 1 and 2 using a MTS procedure. Of course, it is always difficult to place undue weight on null findings, but the two failures to show benefit from an observing-response procedure in a sample with ASD suggests an observing response is not ideal in this situation. It also should be noted that this lack of effect was obtained with participants with ASD who were younger than those tested in Experiments 1 and 2, thus, suggesting a generality to this finding across procedures and age groups.

General Discussion

The experiments reported here showed that participants with ASD display overselectivity in a MTS task (Experiments 1 and 2) and in a simple discrimination learning task (Experiment 3). Although the present results are interpreted as a demonstration that overselectivity was observed in participants with ASD, there was less evidence that the observing response had any effect on that overselectivity. This was true of an observing response without naming (Experiments 1 and 2) and one with naming (Experiment 3). As the initial introduction of an observing response failed to produce a reduction in overselectivity for any study, it is not surprising that the phases intended to investigate the maintenance of such benefit also failed to show a lasting benefit once the intervention had been removed.

Unlike the findings reported in a sample of healthy typically developing adults who were concurrently performing a second, memory task (Broomfield et al., 2007), and those reported in a sample with learning disabilities (Dube & McIlvane, 1999), the observing response did not decrease the level of overselectivity for these participants with ASD. It is not entirely clear why this population did not benefit from the observing-response procedure. It is, of course, possible that the procedure adopted was not adequate to promote sampling of all the elements of the compound stimulus, although the participants were required to point individually to all the elements. More likely is that the procedure is not well suited to a group of individuals (i.e., with ASD) whose behavior is sometimes not easily controlled simultaneously by multiple cues (Koegel & Wilhelm, 1973; Lovaas, Schreibman, Koegel, & Rehm, 1971). Speculatively, it may be that the observing response itself might interfere with the learning of the stimulus elements; that is, there may have been overselectivity between the observing response and the stimulus elements to be learned. In such a situation where an observing response is required, that response, itself, becomes part of the stimulus array (either the sound of the word being said or the image of a pointing finger potentially could configure with the target stimuli). The addition of yet another element into the stimulus complex to be learned about gives further opportunity for overselection, and it may well be the case that this observing-response component of the stimulus array becomes the overselected element given its potential salience. However, the reasons underlying the difficulty for observing-response procedures being successful in a sample of participants with ASD will clearly require further theoretical investigation.

One aspect of the current series of studies that deserves some comment is the range of procedures and samples employed across the three experiments reported here. Although all the experiments employed different procedures, with different probabilities of a response being correct, the observing response failed to affect the behaviors in any procedure. This suggests that the observing response does not work across a range of different settings. Similarly, the samples of children with ASD had somewhat different ages and mental ages (although the autistic severity of the samples used in the three studies was highly similar). These general conclusions also should be weighed against the relatively small sample sizes used in the current studies, which may have limited the power of the studies to detect effect. That such observing effects did not emerge with such sample sizes brings into question their clinical significance.

The literature with respect to the impact of observing responses on overselectivity in ASD is not widely established, although there is little doubt that it can be used for other problems (Constantine & Sidman, 1975; Dube & McIlvane, 1999; Gutowski & Stromer, 2003). But it is possible that it is not useful for learners with ASD, either in a MTS task (Experiments 1 and 2) or in a simple discrimination task (Experiment 3). Given this, the results of the

current studies can be used to provide some support for the suggestion that observing responses are not necessarily the best intervention for overselectivity in individuals with ASD. This conclusion also was drawn by other researchers, who found the use of an observing-response procedure to have an elevating effect on overselectivity, even though the benefit did not last post-intervention.

That the observing-response procedure appears unsuited to these participants with ASD, at least with the current training procedures, will necessitate practitioners using other means to combat overselective responding in individuals with ASD. There are several alternative suggestions that may warrant further investigation in this regard. One finding is that extinction of the previously overselected element can produce an emergence of stimulus control by the previously underselected stimulus with no direct manipulation of the underselected element being necessary (Reed et al., 2008). Alternatively, the use of mindfulness procedure during initial learning has been shown to reduce levels of overselectivity in populations that otherwise show such an effect, such as older people (McHugh, Simpson, & Reed, 2010). This technique might be helpful, at least for individuals with higher functioning autism. Clearly, this is an area that requires further study for important practical purposes.

In terms of the practical implications of these results, aside from speculations regarding potential alternative measures for the reduction of overselective responding, the current findings are used to suggest that teachers should use some caution in the application of observing responses for children with ASD. It may be that such procedures are ineffective, at least with particular individuals, and that, although successful with a range of other behaviors in other disabilities, observing-response procedures may not work with children with ASD.

Acknowledgments

We would like to acknowledge the kind participation of the children in this research, and we thank them very much for their time and involvement. Thanks are also due to the parents of the children who kindly participated and to Lisa A. Osborne for her support.

Declaration of Conflicting Interests

The author(s) declared no potential conflicts of interest with respect to the research, authorship, and/or publication of this article.

Funding

The author(s) received no financial support for the research, authorship, and/or publication of this article.

References

Birnie-Selwyn, B., & Guerin, B. (1997). Teaching children to spell: Decreasing consonant cluster errors by eliminating selective stimulus control. *Journal of Applied Behavior Analysis, 30,* 69–91.

Broomfield, L., McHugh, L., & Reed, P. (2007). The effect of observing response procedures on the reduction of over-selectivity in match to samples tasks: Immediate but not long term benefits. *Research in Developmental Disabilities, 29,* 217–234.

Constantine, B., & Sidman, M. (1975). The role of naming in delayed matching to sample. *American Journal of Mental Deficiency, 79,* 680–689.

Cook, R. A., Anderson, N., & Rincover, A. (1982). Stimulus over-selectivity and stimulus control problems and strategies. In R. L. Kogel, A. Rincover, & A. L. Egel (Eds.), *Educating and understanding autistic children* (pp. 90–105). San Diego, CA: College Hill Press.

Dube, W. V., & McIlvane, W. J. (1999). Reduction of stimulus overselectivity with non-verbal differential observing responses. *Journal of Applied Behavior Analysis, 32,* 25–33.

Dunn, L., Dunn, L., Whetton, C., & Pintile, D. (1982). *The British Picture Vocabulary Scale.* Windsor, UK: NFER Nelson.

Gutowski, S. J., & Stromer, R. (2003). Delayed matching to two pictures samples by individuals with and without disabilities: An analysis of the role of naming. *Journal of Applied Behavior Analysis, 36,* 487–505.

Koegel, R. L., & Wilhelm, H. (1973). Selective responding to the components of multiple visual cues by autistic children. *Journal of Experimental Child Psychology, 15,* 442–453.

Krug, D. A., Arick, J., & Almond, P. (1980). Behavior checklist for identifying severely handicapped individuals with high levels of autistic behavior. *Journal of Child Psychology and Psychiatry, 21,* 221–229.

Lovaas, O. I., & Schreibman, L. (1971). Stimulus overselectivity of autistic children in a two stimulus situation. *Behavior, Research and Therapy, 9,* 305–310.

Lovaas, O. I., Schreibman, L., Koegel, R., & Rehm, R. (1971). Selective responding by autistic children to multiple sensory input. *Journal of Abnormal Psychology, 77,* 211–222.

McHugh, L., & Reed, P. (2007). Age trends in stimulus over-selectivity. *Journal of the Experimental Analysis of Behavior, 88,* 369–380.

McHugh, L., Simpson, A., & Reed, P. (2010). Mindfulness as a potential intervention for stimulus over-selectivity in older adults. *Research in Developmental Disabilities, 31,* 178–184.

Reed, P., Broomfield, L., McHugh, L., McCausland, A., & Leader, G. (2008). Extinction of over-selected stimuli causes emergence of under-selected cues in higher functioning children with Autistic Spectrum Disorders. *Journal of Autism and Developmental Disorders, 39,* 290–298.

Reed, P., & Gibson, E. (2005). The effect of concurrent task load on stimulus overselectivity. *Journal of Autism and Developmental Disorders, 35,* 601–614.

Reynolds, B. S., Newsom, C. D., & Lovaas, O. I. (1974). Auditory over selectivity in autistic children. *Journal of Abnormal Psychology, 2,* 253–263.

Shaffer, D., Lucas, C. P., & Richters, J. E. (1999). *Diagnostic assessment in child and adolescent psychopathology.* New York, NY: Guilford.

Stromer, R., McIlvane, W. J., Dube, W. V., & Mackay, H. A. (1993). Assessing control by elements of complex stimuli in delayed matching to samples. *Journal of the Experimental Analysis of Behavior, 59,* 83–102.

Varni, J. W., Lovaas, O. I., Kogel, R. L, & Everett, N. L. (1979). An analysis of observational learning in autistic and normal children. *Journal of Abnormal Psychology, 7,* 31–43.

Volkmar, F. R., Cicchetti, D. V., Dykens, E., Sparrow, S. S., Leckman, J. F., & Cohen, D. J. (1988). An evaluation of the Autism Behavior Checklist. *Journal of Autism and Developmental Disorders, 18,* 81–97.

Wyckoff, L. B. (1952). The role of observing responses in discriminative learning: Part 1. *Psychological Review, 59,* 431–442.

HAMMILL INSTITUTE
ON DISABILITIES

Focus on Autism and Other
Developmental Disabilities
27(4) 247–253
© 2012 Hammill Institute on Disabilities
Reprints and permission:
sagepub.com/journalsPermissions.nav
DOI: 10.1177/1088357612454917
http://foa.sagepub.com

Comparing Neuropsychological Profiles Between Girls With Asperger's Disorder and Girls With Learning Disabilities

Megan E. McKnight, BS[1,2] and Vincent P. Culotta, PhD[2]

Abstract

Research examining neuropsychological profiles of girls with Asperger's disorder (AD) is sparse. In this study, we sought to characterize neurocognitive profiles of girls with AD compared to girls with learning disabilities (LD). Two groups of school-age girls referred for neuropsychological assessment participated in the study. A total of 23 girls with AD were compared to 50 girls with LD using intellectual, academic, neuropsychological, and behavioral assessments. Standard two-tailed *t*-tests revealed statistically significant discrepancies in a number of areas, and results were interpreted to conclude that the participants with AD had a more severe cognitive and behavioral presentation than same-age girls with LD. The severity of these discrepancies indicates the need for routine neuropsychological and behavioral screening to promote early diagnosis and intervention. Based on this study, we challenge the idea that girls present with a more benign expression of AD than boys.

Keywords

Asperger's disorder, autism spectrum disorders, neuropsychological profile, cortical underconnectivity, learning disabilities

Asperger's disorder (AD) is an autism spectrum disorder (ASD) characterized by predictable deficits in social reciprocity, communication, and repetitive ritualized or restrictive interests and behaviors. On a functional level, youth with AD often evidence awkwardness or oddities in communication despite age-appropriate language acquisition. Such youth have difficulty reading the behaviors of others, may have a preference for predictability, and also may have a tendency toward specific and intense interests (Bolick, 2004). Bolick's (2004) description also indicates inefficient organization and productivity despite reasonably strong intelligence, difficulty integrating sensory information, and predictable problems regulating mood and anxiety. There has been a dramatic increase in the number of youth diagnosed with ASD throughout the past decade (Wilkinson, 2008), that has consistently reflected a gender gap with boys identified at rates substantially higher than those of girls (Wilkinson, 2008).

There is little empirical research characterizing the neuropsychological, academic, and behavioral profiles of girls with AD. Some authors have suggested that girls evidence a milder presentation or form of the disorder (Mattila et al., 2007). Other researchers have suggested that girls experience a delay in diagnosis and may be at risk for underidentification. For example, Wilkinson (2008) found that boys are referred 10 times as much as girls with regard to a possible AD diagnosis. The gender gap in diagnosis, suspected underidentification, and late diagnosis in girls with AD necessitate a greater understanding of the impact of this neurodevelopmental disorder in girls and merits descriptive and prospective research.

The exact cause and mechanism of AD are unknown; however, the prevailing theory that has become a primary focus of autism researchers in recent years is cortical underconnectivity (Just, Cherkassky, Keller, Kana, & Minshew, 2006). The fundamental basis of this theory is a concept of developmental disconnection, suggesting that higher order processing areas of the brain, typically mediated by frontal structures, fail to develop a level of integration necessary to support typical neurodevelopment. The resulting impairment of ability to integrate information can be characterized

[1]The Pennsylvania State University, University Park, USA
[2]Neurobehavioral Associates, Columbia, MD, USA

Corresponding Author:
Vincent P. Culotta, PhD, Neurobehavioral Associates, 5565 Sterrett
Pl #320, Columbia, MD 21044, USA
Email: vculotta@nbatests.com

by behaviors associated with autism as well as cognitive deficits (Cherkassky, Kana, Keller, & Just, 2006).

Similarly, theories underlying the causality of learning disabilities (LD), particularly dyslexia, focus on convergent research indicating hypoactivation and diminished connectivity in regions specific to language processing, sound symbol association, and rapid word form recognition (Gabrieli, 2009). Although both disorders manifest quite differently in children, mechanisms of cortical underconnectivity and diminished activation, with greater regional specificity in LD, may be evident.

Our aim was to depict and describe the intellectual, academic, neuropsychological, and behavioral profiles specific to girls with AD. Despite the presumption of a milder presentation of the disorder for girls than for boys, we hypothesized that girls with AD would demonstrate more significant neurodevelopmental and behavioral discrepancies when compared with same-age girls identified with LD. Documentation of the clinical presentation of AD in girls is imperative to more accurately recognize, diagnose, and treat them.

Method

Participants

Case reports of 23 school-age girls consecutively referred for neuropsychological assessment and subsequently diagnosed solely with AD, based on test scores and direct examination with a pediatric neuropsychologist, were reviewed. The girls ranged in age from 7 years to 21 years, with a mean age of 12 years 5 months.

The comparison group consisted of 50 school-age girls consecutively referred for neuropsychological assessment and subsequently diagnosed with LD, based on test scores and direct examination by a pediatric neuropsychologist. Girls with LD ranged in age from 5 years to 23 years, with a mean age of 12 years 4 months.

Medical, behavioral, and family histories were collected at the time of the evaluation for both groups of girls. Excluded from the study were girls who had a known history of premature birth, neurologic insult, intellectual disability, and/or comorbid diagnoses of attention-deficit/hyperactivity disorder (ADHD) or anxiety disorder.

To assess intellectual, academic, neuropsychological, and behavioral functioning, the second author, a pediatric neuropsychologist, and staff in his office, administered the following evaluative measures:

- *Wechsler Intelligence Scale for Children* (WISC-IV, Wechsler, 2003),
- *Woodcock–Johnson Tests of Achievement–III* (WJ III; Woodcock, McGrew, & Mather, 2001),
- *Grooved Pegboard Test* (GPB; Kløve, 1963),

- *Developmental Test of Visual-Motor Integration* (VMI; Beery & Butenica, 1997),
- *Rey–Osterrieth Complex Figure Test* (RCF; Osterrieth, 1944),
- *Wide Range Assessment of Memory and Learning– Second Edition* (WRAML-2; Sheslow & Adams, 2003),
- *Controlled Oral Word Association Test* (COWA; Benton & Hamsher, 1989),
- *Category Fluency Test* (CFT; Benton & Hamsher, 1989), and
- *Child Behavior Checklist–Parent Form* (CBCL; Achenbach & Rescorla, 2001).

Data Analysis

Scores on measures of intellectual, academic, neuropsychological, and behavioral functioning were compared between the two groups of girls. A standard two-tailed *t*-test was used to assess the significance, if any, of discrepancies between psychometric data for the group of girls with AD when compared with the group of girls with LD.

Results

Intellectual Functioning

Intelligence was assessed via the WISC-III or WISC-IV. Scores tabulated by diagnosis included Verbal IQ, Performance IQ, and Full Scale IQ (FSIQ) composite scores and the Verbal Comprehension, Perceptual Organization, Freedom From Distractibility, Word Memory, and Processing Speed indices (Wechsler, 2003). The Global Assessment of Functioning (GAF) from the *Diagnostic and Statistical Manual of Mental Disorders* (4th ed., text rev.; *DSM-IV-TR*; American Psychiatric Association, 2000) formulation also was included. Mean scores for the groups were compared and significant discrepancies were noted, as shown in Table 1.

The two-tailed *t*-test revealed statistically significant discrepancies between the scores of the AD group and the LD group, with the AD group exhibiting significantly higher scores in the areas of Verbal IQ and Verbal Comprehension Index (VCI), but lower in GAF and Processing Speed.

Academic Functioning

Academic functioning was assessed by comparing the WJ III scores for the Broad and Cluster Reading, Math, and Written Language subtests. Mean Broad scores for both groups are found in Table 2. Two-tailed *t*-test results yielded no statistically significant differences in academic skills, comparing Broad Reading, Math, and Written Language scores. There was an expected trend for stronger reading skills in the girls with AD.

Table 1. Intellectual Ability by Diagnosis

Measure	Girls with SLD			Girls with AD			Difference	Difference ratio	T-score	P
	Score	SD	Count	Score	SD	Count				
WISC composite scores										
Verbal IQ	101.0	14.1	30	110.0	8.4	11	9.2	1.1	2.0	.049*
Performance IQ	98.9	14.4	29	107.0	12.0	10	7.7	1.1	1.5	.014
FSIQ	106.0	11.4	48	106.0	13.0	22	−0.2	1.0	0.1	.921
WISC indexes										
Verbal Comprehension	104.0	13.7	40	112.0	16.0	23	8.6	1.1	2.3	.025*
Perceptional Organizational	106.0	10.8	48	107.0	11.0	23	0.6	1.0	0.2	.842
Freedom From Distractibility	95.5	16.9	13	105.0	8.1	3	9.1	1.1	0.9	.383
Word Memory	100.0	11.6	38	99.9	14.0	20	−0.4	1.0	0.1	.921
Processing Speed	99.5	15.0	48	92.3	13.0	23	−7.2	0.9	2.0	.049*
GAF	65.1	3.95	47	56.3	5.0	23	−8.8	0.9	7.9	.000***

Note: SLD = specific learning disability; AD = Asperger's disorder; WISC = *Wechsler Intelligence Scale for Children*; FSIQ = Full Scale IQ; GAF = Global Assessment of Functioning. Study used the third edition and the fourth edition (WISC-IV; Wechsler, 2003). The GAF is based on the diagnostic formulation from the *Diagnostic and Statistical Manual of Mental Disorders* (4th ed., text rev.; *DSM-IV-TR*; American Psychiatric Association, 2000). *p < .05. **p < .01. ***p < .001.

Table 2. Consecutive Evaluations and Subscale Scores From the WJ III

WJ III scores	Girls with SLD			Girls with AD			Difference	T-score	p value
	Average	SD	No. of data	Average	SD	No. of data			
Broad Reading	98.4	14.7	39	104.0	13	23	−5.8	1.6	.115
Broad Math	102.0	14.5	50	98.1	16	23	3.4	0.9	.371
Broad Written Language	104.0	14.6	40	102.0	15	14	2.5	0.6	.585

Note: WJ III = *Woodcock–Johnson Tests of Achievement–III* (Woodcock, McGrew, & Mather, 2001); SLD = specific learning disability; AD = Asperger's Disorder.

Neuropsychological Functioning

Neuropsychological functioning was assessed using scores from the GPB (dominant and nondominant hand), VMI, RCF (Copy and Delayed), COWA, CFT, and WRAML-2 (Verbal, Story, and Sentence). Girls with AD had significantly higher scores on the WRAML-2 Sentence subtest, but significantly lower scores on the GPB test for the dominant and nondominant hands, and on the VMI.

Behavioral Functioning

The presence and severity of behavioral issues were assessed using the parent version of the CBCL, and the pediatric neuropsychologist's use of the GAF from the *DSM-IV-TR* diagnostic formulation. The two-tailed *t*-test revealed multiple statistically significant differences between the mean scores for the two groups of girls. The AD group had significantly higher scores on seven of the eight syndrome scales and five of the six *DSM*-oriented scales. The scale exhibiting the greatest discrepancy was *Social Problems*. The scale exhibiting the least discrepancy was *Delinquent Behavior*, for which there were no significant differences between the two groups.

Discussion

Our aim in this study was to describe neuropsychological profiles of school-age girls diagnosed with AD and to compare these profiles with those of same-age girls diagnosed with LD. We hypothesized that there would be significant discrepancies among intellectual, academic, neuropsychological, and behavioral measures. We also hypothesized the girls with AD would evidence more significant deficits across these measures given the diffuse nature of their neurodevelopmental disorder. This hypothesis was based on literature in the field indicating the pervasiveness of the effects of ASD on multiple domains of function. We also believed that girls with AD could be differentiated along

Table 3. CBCL and GAF Categories by Diagnosis

Scale	Girls with SLD			Girls with AD			Difference	T-score	Significant (p < .05)
	Average	SD	No. of data	Average	SD	No. of data			
CBCL syndrome									
Anxiety/Depressed	122	14.5	16	108	14.0	44	14.0	3.5	.001***
Withdrawn	126	16.1	16	105	12.0	44	20.0	5.1	.000***
Somatic Complaints	120	15.8	16	108	13.0	44	12.0	3.1	.003**
Social Problems	128	12.8	16	107	8.7	40	21.0	7.0	.000***
Thought Problems	123	13.2	16	107	8.6	40	16.0	5.3	.000***
Attention Problems	130	14.5	16	108	14.0	44	22.0	5.4	.000***
Rule-Breaking Behavior	111	12.2	16	106	9.1	40	4.8	1.6	.115
Aggressive Behavior	117	12.4	16	104	13.0	44	13.0	3.6	.001***
GAF									
Affective Problems	123	14.7	15	108	13.0	43	15.0	3.9	.000***
Anxiety Problems	121	13.7	15	108	13.0	43	14.0	3.6	.001***
Somatic Problems	117	14.8	15	108	13.0	43	9.0	2.2	.032*
ADHD Problems	123	10.7	15	106	14.0	43	16.0	4.1	.000***
Oppositional/Defiant Problems	120	13.2	15	104	12.0	43	16.0	4.3	.000***
Conduct Problems	113	13.1	15	107	11.0	40	6.8	1.9	.062

Note: CBCL = *Child Behavior Checklist–Parent Form* (Achenbach & Rescorla, 2001); GAF = Global Assessment of Functioning (American Psychiatric Association, 2000); SLD = specific learning disability; AD = Asperger's disorder; ADHD = attention-deficit/hyperactivity disorder.
*p < .05. **p < .01. ***p < .001.

various developmental domains compared with normative test values reflecting typically developing girls.

We interpreted the results of the study to support our hypothesis regarding the neuropsychological profiles of girls with AD as compared with girls with LD. Girls with AD exhibited significantly more behavioral problems (see Table 3), which may indicate a deficit in executive functioning. Girls with AD also exhibited significantly lower VCI and verbal intelligence scores (see Tables 1 and 4), which may indicate deficits in verbal memory and verbal fluency. In addition, girls with AD exhibited a significantly lower VMI score (see Table 4), which may indicate deficits in visual construction. Finally, girls with AD exhibited significantly lower scores on the GPB tasks (see Table 4), which may indicate deficits in manual dexterity. They also were more likely to exhibit greater deficits in processing speed, efficiency, and overall behavioral regulation than the girls with LD.

Girls with AD were not significantly different from girls with LD with regard to overall intelligence, academic skills, and select aspects of neuropsychological functioning such as visual memory and perceptual organization skills. Although there were no significant discrepancies between the FSIQs of the AD group and the LD group, girls with AD exhibited higher Verbal IQ and VCI score as measured by the WISC-IV. This group also demonstrated a higher score on the Sentence subtest of the WRAML-2, a measure requiring immediate verbal memory, than girls with LD.

Behaviorally, girls with AD were significantly discrepant from girls with LD on all but one CBCL syndrome scale. Significant discrepancies were evident on scores for *Anxiety/Depressed, Withdrawn, Somatic Complaints, Social Problems,* and *Attention Problems.* There also was a significant discrepancy for *Aggressive Behavior,* with girls with AD having higher scores. The only scale that did not demonstrate a discrepancy was *Delinquent Behavior.*

The most compelling finding of this study is the significant discrepancy observed in the behavioral profile of girls with AD versus girls with LD. This profile suggests that girls with AD have difficulties with internalizing and externalizing behaviors, as well as predictable difficulties with social skills. From a cognitive standpoint, girls with AD demonstrated higher mean Verbal IQ scores compared with those of girls with LD. Academically, the girls with AD were indistinguishable from the girls with LD. This finding is particularly interesting in that one might expect lower scores for girls with LD. The absence of a significant academic discrepancy may suggest that girls with AD generally demonstrate lower levels of academic skill consistent with the profile of girls with LD. From a neurocognitive standpoint, slower fine-motor speed, weaker visual-construction skills, and weaker verbal fluency scores were evident. Weakness in verbal fluency may be particularly important as this skill has a more direct impact on conversational give and take and, ultimately, social skills.

With regard to emerging theories of causality related to AD and autism, the diffuse nature of deficits spanning cognitive, neuropsychological, and behavioral domains may reflect diminished neural integration as posited by theorists

Table 4. Neuropsychological Evaluations by Diagnosis

Evaluation	Girls with SLD			Girls with AD			Difference	T-score	Significant (p < .05)
	Average	SD	No. of data	Average	SD	No. of data			
GPB									
Dominant hand	85.8	22.6	19	104.7	13.0	41	18.9	4.1	.000***
Nondominant hand	88.8	19.6	19	101.8	15.8	41	13.0	2.7	.009**
VMI	82.2	13.0	15	97.7	12.4	22	15.5	3.7	.001***
RCF									
Copy	73.1	20.4	17	83.3	22.9	37	10.2	1.6	.112
Delayed	77.6	20.5	17	83.7	18.5	36	6.1	1.1	.276
CFT	94.9	11.8	19	100.4	11.9	49	5.4	1.7	.094
COWA letters	92.9	22.5	19	92.7	20.2	44	−0.2	0.0	1.000
WRAML-2									
Verbal learning	95.0	12.5	8	101.6	16.9	19	6.6	1.0	.327
Story memory	104.3	18.6	7	96.7	21.7	16	−7.6	0.8	.433
Sentence recall	116.3	12.5	4	97.3	9.8	11	−19.0	3.1	.008**

Note: SLD = specific learning disability; AD = Asperger's disorder; GPB = *Grooved Pegboard Test* (Kløve, 1963); VMI = *Developmental Test of Visual–Motor Integration* (Beery & Butenica, 1997); RCF = *Rey–Osterrieth Complex Figure Test* (Osterrieth, 1944); CFT = *Category Fluency Test* (Benton & Hamsher, 1989); COWA = *Controlled Oral Word Association Test* (Benton & Hamsher, 1989); WRAML-2 = *Wide Range Assessment of Memory and Learning–Second Edition* (Sheslow & Adams, 2003).
*p < .05. **p < .01. ***p < .001.

proposing cortical underconnectivity (Cherkassky et al., 2006). In contrast, researchers examining the neurological underpinnings of LD, particularly dyslexia, suggest a more regionally specific pattern of underactivation and functional disconnections in those tracts relevant to language processing (Gabrieli, 2009). Future research is necessary to link cognitive and behavioral profiles with neuroimaging and genetic studies. Future research also is indicated to understand biological factors governing gender-based differences in AD (Baron-Cohen, 2009).

The results of this study have important implications for identification, diagnosis, and intervention regarding girls with AD. Educators and clinicians should be aware of the more pervasive and diffuse behavioral concerns identified in such girls. Results of our study can be interpreted to indicate the importance of a comprehensive assessment to identify anticipated cognitive weaknesses that may affect academic productivity and exacerbate social functioning. These findings may contribute to an increased recognition of the complexity of issues facing young girls with AD and provide a means to discriminate such girls from girls with LD.

Accommodations, Modifications, and Strategies

In light of these findings and recognizing the impact that cognitive and behavioral regulation and difficulties have on girls with AD in school environments, the following accommodations, modifications, and strategies are suggested. We have grouped these suggestions into accommodations/

modifications that the teacher may offer the student (Teacher–Student), modifications that should travel with the student from class to class (Academic), and strategies that may be implemented either schoolwide or directly with the girls with AD to promote successful behavioral regulation and overall academic and social functioning.

Teacher–student interventions.

- Avoid implicit directions or task constructions.
- Avoid abstract language, inferences, and idiomatic language.
- Do not rely on nonverbal cues to communicate a message or direction.
- Use visual supports, repetition, and checks for comprehension, given weaknesses in verbal memory.
- Cue the student prior to calling on her to allow extra processing time and the ability to formulate an oral response.
- Recognize students' areas of interest and allow opportunities to showcase their knowledge.
- Girls may require observation or facilitation of social interactions during less structured times of day, such as lunch or before/after school.
- Encourage girls with AD to participate in clubs or organizations that offer a high degree of acceptance and support, and a nonjudgmental atmosphere (drama, peer mediation, and service groups may be a great place to start).
- Consider peer mentoring, although this must be done in a thoughtful and well-planned manner.

- Identify a point person or mentor on staff who may be available for periodic check-ins and problem solving for difficult social or academic situations.
- Offer faculty training in social thinking strategies (e.g., Winner, 2005).

Academic interventions.

- Provide extended time on testing to accommodate for diminished processing speed. This may be particularly important in establishing a basis for extended time on high-stakes testing such as the SAT or ACT.
- Offer prereading and prewriting rubrics to support organization and executive function.
- Break down longer assignments into smaller segments with more frequent feedback to accommodate weaknesses in executive functioning.
- Check to ensure that the girl with AD comprehends task instructions.
- Recognize that the curriculum contains increasing amounts of inferential, conceptual, and abstract information as students progress through middle school. This may require greater scaffolding to support comprehension of more abstract concepts.
- Allow girls with AD to leave the room if anxiety necessitates a break from class.
- Consider preferential seating near those students who may be appropriate language, gender, or social models.

Social interventions and cognitive behavioral strategies. The significant elevations in aspects of behavioral regulation may reflect the difficulty girls with AD experience in navigating the academic and social demands of a school setting. Many girls with AD do not feel part of the school's social fabric and may experience persistent symptoms of anxiety that further aggravate cognitive and social weaknesses. Strategies to promote behavioral regulation may include the following:

- Create an environment that appreciates the strengths and weaknesses of girls with AD. This may include staff training by local professionals, involvement of the school psychologist, or the efforts of a local advocacy group.
- Girls with AD may benefit from evidence-based cognitive behavioral strategies in the management of anxiety. These strategies may include thought stopping, self-verbalization, self-calming, and relaxation.
- Some schools have implemented Mindfulness programs based on the work of Kabat-Zinn (2005) to promote self-calming and meditation.

- Because bullying is a problem often encountered by girls with AD in middle or early high school settings, bully-proof training for faculty is recommended. It is also important to recognize that (a) girls with AD may be reluctant to identify themselves as victims of bullying, and (b) bullying may be much more subtle in girls than is evident in boys.
- If the student has an individual education plan (IEP) or a 504 plan, there should be provisions to recognize triggers to anxiety or loss of behavioral control. Some girls with AD may require a Functional Behavioral Assessment and Behavioral Intervention Plan, which are more formal means for addressing behaviors that may interfere with academic or social functioning.
- Medication may be an appropriate tool for some girls with AD. Medication may be used to reduce anxiety, reduce impulsivity, or strengthen aspects of executive functioning such as attention and working memory. The school nurse and appropriate faculty should be made aware of any medication issues.
- It may be helpful to identify a physical space where the girl with AD can go if she is feeling overwhelmed or anxious. This space should allow some privacy—with monitoring—in which a student can employ stress-reducing strategies such as drawing, meditating, listening to music, reading, and so forth.
- Friendship groups, lunch bunches, and other adult-facilitated opportunities for socialization may be helpful. Such groups should be monitored for their efficacy.
- Provide opportunities for girls with AD to explore and develop their specific interests. This may be accomplished through classroom-based projects, extra-credit opportunities, or greater autonomy in choosing topics for papers and projects.
- Accommodations and interventions may be provided through the context of an IEP, a 504 plan, or some form of a student action plan. In any event, it is important that there be a written plan to facilitate students' academic and social progress and avoid the difficulties identified in this study.

Strengths and Limitations

Strengths of this study include an empirical assessment of girls with AD, given the paucity of such research. Additional strengths include the sample size given the low prevalence of girls diagnosed with AD. The LD control group also was of considerable size and strength.

The broad strength of this study is that it contributes to a very small body of research concerning the clinical presentation of girls with AD. The results are interpreted to demonstrate that these girls present in a similar way as girls with LD, and may be useful in making more accurate diagnoses.

Weaknesses of this study include its retrospective design, absence of greater sociodemographic features associated with the sample size, and participant selection from a group of youth specifically referred for assessment.

Declaration of Conflicting Interests

The author(s) declared no potential conflicts of interest with respect to the research, authorship, and/or publication of this article.

Funding

The author(s) received no financial support for the research, authorship, and/or publication of this article.

References

Achenbach, T. M., & Rescorla, L. A. (2001). *Manual for the ASEBA school-age forms and profiles*. Burlington: University of Vermont, Research Center for Children, Youth, and Families.

American Psychiatric Association. (2000). *Diagnostic and statistical manual of mental disorders* (4th ed., text rev.). Washington, DC: Author.

Baron-Cohen, S. (2009). Autism: The empathizing-systemizing (E-S) theory. *Annals of the New York Academy of Sciences, 1156*, 68–80.

Beery, K. E., & Butenica, N. A. (1997). *Developmental Test of Visual Motor Integration*. Odessa, FL: Psychological Assessment.

Benton, A. L., & Hamsher, K. D. (1989). *Multilingual aphasia examination*. Iowa City, IA: AJA Associates.

Bolick, T. (2004). *Asperger syndrome and adolescence: Helping preteens and teens get ready for the real world*. Gloucester, MA: Fair Winds.

Cherkassky, V., Kana, R., Keller, T., & Just, M. A. (2006). Functional connectivity in a baseline resting-state network in autism. *Neuroreport, 17*, 1687–1690.

Gabrieli, J. (2009). Dyslexia: A new synergy between education and cognitive neuroscience. *Science, 325*, 280–283.

Just, M., Cherkassky, T., Keller, R., Kana, K., & Minshew, N. (2006). Functional and anatomical cortical underconnectivity in autism: Evidence from an FMRI study of an executive function task and corpus callosum morphometry. *Cerebral Cortex, 174*, 951–961.

Kabat-Zinn, J. (2005). *Wherever you go, there you are: Mindfulness meditation in everyday life*. New York, NY: Hyperion.

Kløve, H. (1963). Clinical neuropsychology. In F. M. Forster (Ed.), *The medical clinics of North America* (pp. 1647–1658). New York, NY: Saunders.

Mattila, M. L., Kielinen, M., Jussila, K., Linna, S., Bloigu, R., Ebeling, H., & Moilanen, I. (2007). An epidemiological and diagnostic study of Asperger syndrome according to four sets of diagnostic criteria. *Journal of the American Academy of Child & Adolescent Psychiatry, 46*, 636–646.

Osterrieth, P. A. (1944). Filetest de copie d'une figure complex: Contribution a l'etude de la perception et de la memoire [The test of copying a complex figure: A contribution to the study of perception and memory]. *Archives de Psychologie, 30*, 286–356.

Sheslow, D., & Adams, W. (2003). *Wide Range Assessment of Memory and Learning–Second Edition: Administration and technical manual*. Lutz, FL: Psychological Assessment.

Wechsler, D. (2003). *Wechsler Intelligence Scale for Children–Fourth Edition* (WISC-IV). San Antonio, TX: Psychological Corporation.

Wilkinson, L. (2008). The gender gap in Asperger syndrome: Where are the girls? *Teaching Exceptional Children Plus, 4*, 1–10.

Winner, M. G. (2005). *Think Social! A social thinking curriculum for school-age students for teaching social thinking and related social skills to students with high functioning autism, Asperger syndrome, PDD-NOS, ADHD, nonverbal learning disability and for all others in the murky gray area of social thinking*. San Jose, CA: Think Social.

Woodcock, R. W., McGrew, K. W., & Mather, N. (2001). *Woodcock-Johnson III*. Itasca, IL: Riverside.

HAMMILL INSTITUTE
ON DISABILITIES

Focus on Autism and Other
Developmental Disabilities
27(4) 254–262
© 2012 Hammill Institute on Disabilities
Reprints and permission:
sagepub.com/journalsPermissions.nav
DOI: 10.1177/1088357612457989
http://foa.sagepub.com

Children With Autism: Sleep Problems and Symptom Severity

Megan E. Tudor, MA[1], Charles D. Hoffman, PhD[2],
and Dwight P. Sweeney, PhD[2]

Abstract

Relationships between the specific sleep problems and specific behavioral problems of children with autism were evaluated. Mothers' reports of sleep habits and autism symptoms were collected for 109 children with autism. Unlike previous research in this area, only children diagnosed with autism without any commonly comorbid diagnoses (e.g., intellectual disability, epilepsy) were included in the analysis. Consistent with prior work, a positive correlation between the severity of sleep problems and the severity of autism symptoms was obtained. Sleep onset delay and sleep duration were positively correlated with autism symptoms and autism severity. Sleep onset delay was the strongest predictor of communication deficit, stereotyped behavior, and autism severity. These results provide support for specific sleep problem and symptom relationships that are unique to autism and suggest the importance of including the treatment of sleep problems as part of a comprehensive behavioral intervention for children with autism.

Keywords

autism, sleep problems, stereotyped behaviors, communication, social interaction

Children with autism are reported to have a greater prevalence of sleep problems than typically developing children (e.g., Hoffman, Sweeney, Gilliam, & Lopez-Wagner, 2006; Schreck & Mulick, 2000). Parents' reports suggest that 15% to 35% of typically developing children experience sleep problems (Mindell, 1993), with the respective rate for children with autism ranging from 44% to 83% (Richdale, 1999). In a study of young children aged 3 to 5 years, Krakowiak, Goodlin-Jones, Hertz-Picciotto, Croen, and Hansen (2008) suggested that serious sleep problems exist in 53% of children with autism, compared with 46% of children with other developmental disabilities (DDs), and only 32% of typically developing children. These authors also found that children with autism were reported to experience more difficulties with sleep onset and night wakings than children in the comparison groups. Previously, researchers found that children with autism of various ages experience a variety of sleep problems, such as prolonged sleep onset, decreased time asleep, and frequent night wakings (e.g., Allik, Larsson, & Smedje, 2006; Honomichl, Goodlin-Jones, Burnham, Gaylor, & Anders, 2002; Wiggs & Stores, 2004; Williams, Sears, & Allard, 2004).

Maladaptive sleep patterns also are evidenced as a detriment to daytime behavior and cognition in typically developing children (National Institutes of Health, 2003). Disturbed sleep is associated with diminished performance in typically developing children's functioning in areas such as memory, vigilance, and affect (Kheirandish & Gozal, 2006; Sadeh, Gruber, & Raviv, 2002). Significant cognitive delays in higher mental functions, such as verbal fluency and abstract thinking, are displayed in typically developing children following just one night of sleep deprivation (Randazzo, Meuhlbach, Schweitzer, & Walsh, 1998). Furthermore, children's sleep-disordered breathing is suggested to be associated with higher rates of inattention, hyperactivity, and aggression (Chervin et al., 2002; Gottlieb, Vezina, & Chase, 2003).

Symptoms for a variety of disorders may be intensified when sleep problems are present. For example, intensified symptoms of attention-deficit/hyperactivity disorder (ADHD) are associated with the sleep problems of these children, with symptoms appearing to intensify when sleep problems were reported (Corkum, Tannock, Moldofsky, Hogg-Johnson, & Humphries, 2001). A sample of children with the general diagnosis of intellectual disability (ID) demonstrated worsened cognitive dysfunction when severe sleep problems were present (Didden, Korzilius, van Aperlo, van

[1]Stony Brook University, NY, USA
[2]California State University, San Bernardino, USA

Corresponding Author:
Megan E. Tudor, MA, Department of Psychology, Stony Brook University, Stony Brook, NY 11794-2500, USA
Email: metudor@notes.cc.sunysb.edu

Overloop, & de Vries, 2002). Evidence also suggests that intensified problem behavior is associated with sleep problems in children with pervasive developmental disorders (PDD; Patzold, Richdale, & Tonge, 1998). DeVincent, Gadow, Delosh, and Geller (2007) documented differential sleep–behavior relationships for young children with PDD and for typically developing children. Both groups of children were reported to have higher rates of problem behavior when sleep problems were concurrently reported. Specifically, all children with sleep problems reportedly showed more aggression, hyperactivity, distraction, and defiance than children who did not experience sleep problems. However, children with PDD were found to exhibit more overall severe sleep disturbance and inappropriate behavior than typically developing children. These findings collectively suggest a strong relationship between sleep problems and behavioral symptoms seen in children with a variety of DDs. The notion that sleep problems exacerbate daytime symptoms is possible but unclear based on the reported correlations. Notably, the sleep–symptom relationships described above represent behavioral or medical diagnoses that are either highly comorbid or diagnostically inherent to a diagnosis of autism.

Research has been conducted with regard to the relationship between sleep problems and children's autism symptoms. In 2004, Schreck, Mulick, and Smith used the Behavioral Evaluation of Disorders of Sleep (Schreck & Mulick, 2000) and the *Gilliam Autism Rating Scale* (GARS; Gilliam, 1995) to examine the potential relationship between parents' reports of their children's sleep problems and autism symptoms. The GARS subscales represented the triad of symptom severity for stereotyped behavior, communication, and social interaction, as well as developmental disturbance. Overall, autism severity was represented by the autism index (AI), derived from the cumulative scores on the aforementioned GARS subscales. Parents' reports of sleep problem severity were found to be positively correlated with their reports of their children's autism symptom severity. In addition, short sleep duration was found to be the best sleep problem predictor for overall autism severity and also predicted stereotyped behavior and social skills deficits subscales scores. Both the Expressive Awakening and High Sensitivity to Environmental Stimuli subscales were related to children's communication deficit. These findings are interpreted to suggest that sleep problems may exacerbate autism symptoms and that there are specific relationships found among these sleep problems and autism symptoms.

Hoffman et al. (2005) also used parent reports on the GARS (Gilliam, 1995) to assess severity of autism symptoms in a larger sample of children with autism. To measure sleep problems, the researchers used the widely used Children's Sleep Habits Questionnaire (CSHQ; Owens, Spirito, & McGuinn, 2000). In line with the previous research,

significant relationships between mothers' reports of their children's sleep problems and their report of their children's autism severity were found. Results indicated that sleep-disordered breathing was positively correlated with overall severity of autism scores as well as GARS subscales assessing stereotyped behavior and social interaction deficits. In addition, parasomnias (such as night terrors) were found to predict developmental disturbance. The authors suggested that future research in this area should endeavor to control for comorbid DD diagnoses, which may confound the sleep–autism symptom relationships. Similarly, in a meta-analysis, Richdale and Schreck (2009) recommended that future studies use controlled sampling that excludes the various DD diagnoses that are related to autism.

The aim for the current study was to examine the relationships between sleep problems and autism symptoms in a sample of children with a diagnosis of autism but without any comorbid DD diagnoses. Given that a variety of DDs, such as ID (Richdale, Francis, Gavidia-Payne, & Cotton, 2000), ADHD (Corkum et al., 2001), and epilepsy (Cortesi, Giannotti, & Ottaviano, 2005), are commonly comorbid with autism and that these disorders present their own repertoire of related sleep problems (Matson & Nebel-Schwalm, 2005), controlling for comorbid conditions was expected to derive a more accurate assessment of the relationship between sleep problems and symptom severity in children with autism. Given the exploratory design and novel sampling method of the current study, it was expected that a relationship between sleep problem severity and symptom severity would be replicated and that relationships between other sleep problems and autism symptoms would be identified.

Method

Participants

Participants consisted of mother volunteers who were recruited through a treatment and research program. Mothers reported on their children who were independently diagnosed with autism by independent professionals, such as pediatricians and licensed clinical psychologists, which qualified them for state-provided behavioral services. The independent diagnoses were not conducted by any person involved in the current study. All of the participants received treatment at a center-based behavior modification and parental education program located on the campus of an inland southern California university. As consumers of the program, families attended 2.5 hr weekly sessions, with parents attending a counselor-led support group while their children with autism received one-on-one behavioral treatment. The local California State Regional Center provides funding for families to receive such services (California Department of Developmental Services, 2008). The protocol for the current investigation was approved by the Institutional Review Board of the university campus where the study was conducted.

Mothers' reports on the GARS–Second Edition (GARS-2; Gilliam, 2006) and the CSHQ were extracted from a larger archival data set consisting of data collected from families who volunteered to participate in the center's research program. A total of 109 children (18 females and 91 males) out of 402 met the criteria of having an independent diagnosis of autism with no other comorbid DDs or epilepsy. Notably, the sample did not include children with PDD–not otherwise specified (PDD-NOS) or Asperger syndrome. The ages for the children in the present study ranged from 3 to 18 years ($M = 7.06$, $SD = 2.67$). The children's ethnicities were reported as follows: African American/Black, $n = 10$ (9.3%); Asian/Pacific Islander, $n = 10$ (9.3%); Hispanic, $n = 25$ (23.1%); Middle Eastern, $n = 1$ (0.9%); Native American, $n = 2$ (1.9%); White/Caucasian, $n = 42$ (38.9%); and Mixed or Other, $n = 16$ (14.8%).

Measures

CSHQ. The CSHQ is a parent-report survey used to identify behavioral and medical sleep habits and problems in school-aged children (Owens et al., 2000). The measure includes 45 items that represent prominent sleep difficulties and prevalent diagnostic symptom severity for pediatric sleep disorders (American Sleep Disorders Association, 1990). The CSHQ consists of eight subscales of sleep problems frequently experienced by children (Owens et al., 2000): Bedtime Resistance, Sleep Onset Delay, Sleep Duration (e.g., not getting enough hours of sleep per night), Sleep Anxiety, Night Wakings, Parasomnias (e.g., sleep apnea, night terrors, restless leg syndrome), Sleep-Disordered Breathing, and Daytime Sleepiness. These subscales generate a total sleep disturbance score. Mothers were asked to respond to questions while focusing on their children's most recent and typical week of sleep. Frequencies of certain sleep behaviors displayed by the child are indicated using a 3-point scale: *usually* (5–7 nights per week), *sometimes* (2–4 nights per week), or *rarely* (0–1 night per week). Other items, such as usual bedtime and time of waking, require free response by the parent. The CSHQ has proven useful in numerous studies related to children and their sleep problems, including the study of children with autism spectrum disorders (e.g., Hoffman et al., 2005; Honomichl et al., 2002).

GARS-2. The GARS-2 is a parent-report survey used to evaluate autism based on the diagnostic criteria of the *Diagnostic and Statistical Manual of Mental Disorders* (4th ed.; *DSM-IV*; American Psychiatric Association, 2000) and the Autism Society of America's (1994) definition of the disorder. The three subscales included in the GARS-2 are based on the main domains of symptomology of the disorder: Stereotyped Behaviors, Social Interaction, and Communication. The summation of subscale scores yield the AI, which has a mean of 100 and a standard deviation of 15. The AI score represents an overall estimate of autism severity. According to the GARS-2 test manual (Gilliam, 2006), in a sample of children and adolescents diagnosed with autism ($N = 1,107$), 90% yielded an AI score higher than 85, which indicates a high likelihood of meeting criteria for autism diagnosis. The original version of this measure, the GARS, has been commended as a valid and reliable tool for diagnosis of autism (Filipek et al., 2000; National Research Council, 2001). The GARS-2, used in the current study, includes improvements that were the focus of critique in the earlier form of the measure (Lecavalier, 2005; South et al., 2002). The GARS-2 has been used in several previous studies related to autism symptom severity (e.g., Hoffman et al., 2005; O'Connor & Healy, 2010; Stuart & McGrew, 2009)

For the current study, overall GARS-2 scores for the child participants had a range of 59 to 130 *(M = 93.86, SD = 16.47)*. In this sample, 69% of the children had an AI at or above 85. A total of 30 children who do not use spoken language to communicate did not have a Communication subscale score, as the measure is not sensitive to children who use alternative forms of communication. Therefore, the Communication subscale-related analyses were not representative of children who use sign language, Picture Exchange Communication System (PECS) boards, or other forms of communication beyond verbal speech. Nonetheless, the GARS-2 provides transformation guidelines so that children who communicate nonverbally were still represented in regard to stereotyped behavior, communication, and AI. Limited communication abilities are commonly associated with a lower intelligence quotient and, therefore, ID (e.g., Waterhouse et al., 1996); however, none of the participants in the current study had an independent professional diagnosis of ID.

Procedure

A two-part assessment process preceded enrollment in regular weekly center sessions as part of the behavior and research program described above. This process consisted of behavioral center staff visiting the family's home for a period of approximately 1.5 hr. A trained staff member assisted mothers in their completion of the GARS-2 by explaining the measure and providing clarification of items as requested. Staff did not participate in the actual rating process beyond this level of support to ensure that parents provided an unbiased estimate of their children's behavior. One or two additional staff members observed and interacted with the child to collect baseline behavioral data. Mothers also were presented with information regarding the program and its integrated ongoing research program during the initial session. After being provided with appropriate informed consent and agreeing to participate in the research program, mothers were given a packet of research surveys

Table 1. Pearson Bivariate Correlations for CSHQ and GARS-2 Factors

CSHQ	GARS-2			
	Stereotyped behavior	Communication	Social interaction	AI
Bedtime Resistance	.11	.11	.11	.13
Sleep Onset Delay	.31**	.28*	.40**	.42**
Sleep Duration	.32**	.22*	.33**	.38**
Sleep Anxiety	.08	−.05	.11	.09
Night Wakings	.11	.16	.26**	.15
Parasomnias	.17	.28*	.21*	.26**
Sleep-Disordered Breathing	.15	−.04	.19*	.14
Daytime Sleepiness	.10	.19	.11	.14
Total sleep disturbance score	.24*	.25*	.22*	.32**

Note: CSHQ = Children's Sleep Habits Questionnaire (Owens, Spirito, & McGuinn, 2000); GARS-2 = *Gilliam Autism Rating Scale*–Second Edition (Gilliam, 2006). N = 109.
$*p < .05. **p < .01$.

and questionnaires, including the CSHQ, to complete and return to the center at their earliest convenience. The anonymity (and confidentiality) of these measures was assured for participants, as response packets were identifiable only by a predetermined code number.

Data Analysis

All data were entered separately by two research assistants for error control. Specialized syntax from manuals for the utilized measures were used to compute all scores (Gilliam, 2006; Owens et al., 2000). All data collection and analyses were performed using the Statistical Package for the Social Sciences (2006).

Pearson correlations were performed on scores for the CSHQ and the GARS-2 to examine relationships between sleep problems and autism symptomology. Further analysis was performed using a simultaneous multiple regression model to examine CSHQ sleep problem variables as predictors for each of the GARS-2 subscales as well as for AI scores (the criterion measures). Sleep duration and daytime sleepiness were not used as predictors in the analyses because of their likelihood of being outcomes of actual sleep problems, and not necessarily the sleep problem itself (see Hoffman et al., 2005). Total sleep disturbance was excluded from the analyses as this score comes from and is, therefore, highly correlated with all the other CSHQ subscales. These regressions were further analyzed for partial correlations to reveal which specific sleep problems showed the strongest predictive value for the criterion variables while controlling for the variance of all other predictor variables.

Results

To ensure the integrity of the statistical analyses, the data were screened for missing values, skewness, and kurtosis.

The series mean was imputed for all missing values on the CSHQ subscales; the number or missing values ranged from 3 participants (2%, Sleep Onset Delay) and 21 participants (19%, Bedtime Resistance). Mean imputation is a debated statistical method, yet is appropriate for the current study given that the missing data appear to be nonsystematic and the total number of missing values of any given subscale is relatively low (Acock, 2005). Mean imputation was not performed for the Communication subscale of the GARS-2 given that the absence of a value for this variable indicates that the child possesses no oral communication and, therefore, no transformation could provide a meaningful estimation of their communication abilities. Only one variable (the Sleep-Disordered Breathing subscale of the CSHQ) yielded kurtosis and skewness estimates that slightly exceeded normality assumptions. However, transforming this variable did not result in a change among the correlation and regression values reported below, so the originally reported values were left intact.

Correlations between the eight CSHQ subscales and the three GARS-2 subscales and AI score were calculated. The results of the Pearson bivariate correlations are displayed in Table 1. Sleep Onset Delay, Sleep Duration, and Total Sleep Disturbance were significantly correlated with all autism symptom subscales and overall AI. The Parasomnias subscale was significantly correlated with Communication, Social Interaction, and AI, but not the Stereotyped Behaviors subscale. Finally, Night Wakings and sleep-disordered breathing were significantly correlated with social interaction scores alone but none of the other GARS-2 subscales.

The significant results of the regression model are displayed in Table 2. Separate multiple regression analyses were performed to evaluate CSHQ subscales as predictors and each of the GARS-2 subscales and AI score as the criterion variables. Statistically significant overall regression models were evidenced for each of the four analyses. The

Table 2. Significant Regression and Partial Correlation Values for CSHQ Predictors of GARS-2 Criterion Measures

GARS-2 criterion measures	Overall regression		Significant CSHQ predictors	Partial correlation
	F	R²		
Stereotyped behavior	2.23*	.12	Sleep Onset Delay	.27**
Social interaction	5.05***	.23	Sleep Onset Delay	.38***
			Night wakings	.22*
Communication	2.79*	.19	Sleep Anxiety	.26*
			Parasomnias	.27*
Autism index	4.42***	.210	Sleep Onset Delay	.37***

Note: CSHQ = Children's Sleep Habits Questionnaire (Owens, Spirito, & McGuinn, 2000); GARS-2 = *Gilliam Autism Rating Scale–Second Edition* (Gilliam, 2006). N = 109.
*p < .05. **p < .01. ***p < .001.

included group of CSHQ subscales was shown to significantly predict the magnitude of each of the criterion variables: Stereotyped Behaviors, $F(6, 108) = 2.23$, $p < .05$, $R^2 = .12$; Social Interaction, $F(6, 108) = 5.05$, $p < .001$, $R^2 = .23$; Communication, $F(6, 78) = 2.79$, $p = .05$, $R^2 = .19$; and AI, $F(6, 108) = 4.42$, $p < .001$, $R^2 = .21$.

Subsequent partial correlation analyses were conducted to assess the value of each discrete CSHQ subscale on the criterion GARS-2 subscales. When controlling for all of the variance contributed by other sleep problems, Sleep onset delay ($pr = .27$, $p < .01$) attained the strongest predictive value of the Stereotyped Behaviors subscale. Similarly, sleep onset delay ($pr = .38$, $p < .001$) was shown to be the strongest predictor of the Social Interaction subscale, although night wakings ($pr = .22$, $p < .05$) also emerged as a significantly strong predictor of this criterion variable. Furthermore, sleep anxiety ($pr = -.23$, $p < .05$) and parasomnias ($pr = .27$, $p < .05$) were evidenced as the strongest predictors of the Communication subscale when all other sleep problems were controlled for. Finally, and consistent with the regression models with the Stereotyped Behaviors and Social Interaction subscales as criterion variables, sleep onset delay ($pr = .37$, $p < .001$) was shown as the strongest predictor of AI score or overall autism severity.

Discussion

As anticipated, the current findings are consistent with previous research in that relationships between children's sleep difficulties and their behavioral symptoms were obtained. The results also present new information on precisely how sleep symptoms relate to the severity of autism symptoms. Mothers' reports in the current study, unlike previous work, reflected the sleep problems and symptom severity of children with autism and no comorbid DD diagnoses. The results of the current study are interpreted to corroborate findings of previous researchers to conclude that mothers'

reports of the severity of their children's sleep problems were related to their reports of their children's autism symptom severity. Unprecedented findings were revealed in regard to the specific relationships between sleep problems and symptoms, which was not unexpected given that the current methodological framework was designed to suggest relationships that are unique to autism without comorbid DD diagnoses.

Overall sleep disturbance, problems with sleep onset delay, and short sleep duration were associated with all autism symptoms as well as overall autism severity. These findings suggest that overall lack of sleep is associated with a more severe repertoire of autism symptoms during the day, a finding that is consistent with results obtained with broader samples of children with other DDs (Schreck et al., 2004). Much as the functioning of typically developing children suffers from lack of sleep, children with autism suffer from an increase in stereotyped behavior, social deficits, and communication deficits when sleep is limited.

Sleep onset delay was evidenced as a predictor of stereotyped behavior, social interaction deficit, and overall autism severity, but not as a predictor of communication deficit. Similar to the aforementioned findings regarding restricted sleep duration, the prevalence of sleep onset delay surely also denotes that the children with autism were not getting enough sleep because they were unable to fall asleep for several hours. Therefore, these findings suggest that overall lack of sleep in children with autism, which may be commonly caused by sleep onset delay, may contribute to the intensification of most autism symptoms. It is problematic to draw implications from sleep onset delay's failure to predict communication deficits, given that children without verbal abilities are excluded from the autism severity measure used in the study. It is possible that this methodological concern as well as the truncated range of communication data complicated these results. Nevertheless, the significance of sleep onset delay in relation to the other symptoms further supports this particular sleep problem as a possible intensifier of daytime autism symptoms. The prominence of sleep onset delay as a problem experienced by children with autism has been found in a study that included children with a variety of ASD (Krakowiak et al., 2008) and another study that focused on children with ID and autism (Cotton & Richdale, 2006), but not in previous work that included children with autism and other comorbid DDs (Hoffman et al., 2005).

Parasomnias were significantly related to Stereotyped Behaviors, Communication, and overall autism severity. These associations are consistent with findings for populations with autism and other comorbidities, as is the finding that parasomnias were a significant predictor of communication symptoms; however, previous researchers also found parasomnias to be a predictor of overall autism severity (Hoffman et al., 2005). It has been questioned whether parasomnias are indeed a sleep disorder particular to autism or whether their presence in children with autism is a problem associated with comorbid disorders (Hoffman et al., 2005). According to the current results, parasomnias are present in children with a sole diagnosis of autism and are related to communication deficits. Further study of specific parasomnias that children with autism experience, such as restless leg syndrome and night terrors, is warranted.

Other specific sleep problem–autism symptom relationships were found. Night wakings were associated with communication symptoms. In regard to prediction value, night wakings were demonstrated as a predictor of social interaction symptoms. Night wakings have not been previously noted in significant associations with or as a significant predictor of autism symptoms. Night wakings result in overall less sleep throughout the night, and, as stated above, these results point to a general lack of sleep as an important factor in symptom severity.

A similar pattern of results was shown with sleep-disordered breathing; this sleep problem was associated with communication symptoms. These findings were different from previous findings, where sleep-disordered breathing was indicated as the most prominent associative and predictive factor of all autism symptoms (Hoffman et al., 2005). This suggests that sleep-disordered breathing is not as relevant to populations with autism as it is to populations with other DDs. Sleep-disordered breathing has been shown as a major sleep problem for children with epilepsy and children with ID, both conditions that are often comorbid with autism (Maganti et al., 2006; Wiggs, 2003). Consequently, we believe that the sampling methods of the current study avoided the confounds that may result from a diagnostically diverse sample of children with autism.

Finally, sleep anxiety was a significant predictor of communication symptoms. Specifically, less severe communication symptoms were associated with higher sleep anxiety. This relationship may well be attributable to children with better communication abilities; children with verbal abilities can adequately communicate their fears or anxiety about sleep to their parents. Conversely, children with nonverbal, limited verbal, or otherwise impaired communication abilities were unlikely able to alert their parents to sleep anxiety problems. Parents may interpret sleep anxiety as noncompliance or other forms of problem behavior. Unlike the obvious and observable problem of their children not sleeping, sleep anxiety may be an internalized sleep problem that is reported only by parents who have children who are capable of communicating with them. Relationships between anxiety and sleep problems have been noted in a previous sample of children with various autism spectrum disorders (Wiggs & Stores, 2004) and a sample of children with Asperger syndrome (Paavonen et al., 2008). Past work, in combination with the current findings, cannot help clarify whether sleep anxiety is a sleep problem that is unique to children with

verbal abilities, who also are more likely to have higher intellectual abilities (Ritvo & Freeman, 1978), and further study is warranted.

According to the findings of this study, the prolonged time needed for children with autism to fall asleep and their overall lack of sleep may intensify their symptoms in most symptom areas. Therefore, it is important to consider how to treat these sleep problems in this population. Sleep hygiene has been suggested as a behavioral method of improving sleep for typically developing children and children with DDs (Hoban, 2000). These methods include parental involvement in establishing bedtime routines, a sleep-conducive environment, and being wary of giving the child any unintentional reinforcement for staying awake. Indeed, positive behavioral strategies have been shown to decrease night waking and overall problematic sleep experienced by children with autism (Christodulu & Durand, 2004). The necessity of empirically based sleep intervention is especially important given that parent accommodation of maladaptive sleep patterns has been cited as strong predictors of sleep problems for children with autism (Liu, Hubbard, Fabes, & Adam, 2006), which may exacerbate mothers' stress and personal sleep problems (Hoffman et al., 2008). Furthermore, pharmacological treatments, such as melatonin, are supported as effective sleep treatment for many children with autism (for a review, see Guénolé et al., 2011).

These options for alleviating and assessing sleep problems should be considered as part of an overall treatment plan, given the evidence that sleep problems exacerbate daytime behavioral symptoms of children with autism, which may in turn affect response to treatment and various other activities of daily living. Sleep problems, like physical pain or emotional distress, could be considered a "setting event" that can trigger problem behavior for children with autism (Carr, 1992). If sleep problems are weighted as a setting event for autism symptoms, a more comprehensive and effective individually tailored treatment program can be made for each child with autism.

Furthermore, future research in this field requires more in-depth inspection of the actual sleep problems and symptoms of children with autism. The current and many related studies have relied on parent reports; less subjective measures could enhance our knowledge in this field. Use of actigraphy to physiologically measure the children's sleep might be helpful in identifying sleep habits in a nonsubjective and noninvasive manner (Allik et al., 2006; Oyane & Bjorvatn, 2005). Wearing an actigraphic wristband has proven an effective measure of sleep problems in samples of children with autism (Goodlin-Jones et al., 2009; Schwichtenberg, Iosif, Goodlin-Jones, Tang, & Anders, 2011; Wiggs & Stores, 2004) and is an appealing approach to sleep measurement with this population, as children with autism often have heightened sensitivity to sensory stimuli that makes invasive measurements inoperable. Furthermore, polysomnographic techniques combined with video monitoring have been an effective means of measuring sleep problems for children with autism (Elia et al., 2000; Malow et al., 2006). In addition to these types of sleep measurements, a more objective and observational means of measuring children's symptoms would greatly benefit this area of research. In addition to improvements on sleep measurement in children with autism, the need for multiple indicators of specific diagnoses should be addressed in future research. Here, professional independent diagnoses were used to define our sample, which is more objective than the typical parent-report approach to diagnosis. Nevertheless, multiple professional and standardized sources that corroborate on specific autism and comorbid diagnoses, as well as medication regimens, are keys for understanding the differential relationships between sleep and psychopathology.

In conclusion, we suggest that children with autism experience specific sleep problem–autism symptom relationships that have not been evidenced in previous research and may not exist in populations with other diagnoses that are commonly comorbid with or inherent to autism, which is of great import to the clinical issues and future research related to this field. Further research examining these relationships, using multiple indicators of the disorder as well as more objective indices of children's sleep difficulties, are suggested. The results of the current study evidence the importance of treatments that aid in the research that focuses on the sleep health of children with autism, with direct consideration of the pattern of individual sleep problems and unique symptom severity of each child. Such information is invaluable, as any means that assist children with autism to sleep better could, in turn, help reduce symptom severity. Therefore, targeting sleep problems as part of intervention plans may increase interaction and response to intervention, and improve the quality of life for children with autism and their family members.

Acknowledgment

The authors would like to thank Tanner M. Carollo, MA, for his assistance in early stages of this project.

Authors' Note

Preliminary results of this study were included in a poster presentation at the April 2009 Western Psychological Association convention in Portland, Oregon. In addition, this study was initially developed as part of the first author's undergraduate honors thesis.

Declaration of Conflicting Interests

The authors declared no potential conflicts of interest with respect to the research, authorship, and/or publication of this article.

Funding

The authors received no financial support for the research, authorship, and/or publication of this article.

References

Acock, A. C. (2005). Working with missing values. *Journal of Marriage and Family, 67*, 1012–1028.

Allik, H., Larsson, J. O., & Smedje, H. (2006). Sleep patterns of school-age children with Asperger syndrome or high-functioning autism. *Journal of Autism and Developmental Disorders, 36*, 585–595.

American Psychiatric Association. (2000). *Diagnostic and statistical manual of mental disorders* (4th ed., text rev.). Washington, DC: Author.

American Sleep Disorders Association. (1990). *International classification of sleep disorders: Diagnostic and coding manual.* Rochester, MN: Author.

Autism Society of America. (1994). Definition of autism. *Advocate: Newsletter of the Autism Society of America, 26*, 3.

California Department of Developmental Services. (2008). *Information about regional centers.* Available from http://www.dds.ca.gov

Carr, E. G. (1992). Emerging themes in the functional analysis of problem behavior. *Journal of Applied Behavior Analysis, 27*, 393–399.

Chervin, R. D., Archbold, K. H., Dillon, J. E., Panahi, P., Pituch, K. J., Dahl, R. E., & Guilleminault, C. (2002). Inattention, hyperactivity, and symptoms of sleep-disordered breathing. *Pediatrics, 109*, 449–456.

Christodulu, K. V., & Durand, V. M. (2004). Reducing bedtime disturbance and night waking using positive bedtime routines and sleep restriction. *Focus on Autism and Other Developmental Disabilities, 19*, 130–139.

Corkum, P., Tannock, R., Moldofsky, H., Hogg-Johnson, S., & Humphries, T. (2001). Actigraphy and parental ratings of sleep in children with attention deficit/hyperactivity disorder. *Sleep, 24*, 3030–3312.

Cortesi, F., Giannotti, F., & Ottaviano, S. (2005). Sleep problems and daytime behavior in childhood idiopathic epilepsy. *Epilepsia, 40*, 1557–1565.

Cotton, S., & Richdale, A. (2006). Brief report: Parental descriptions of sleep problems in children with autism, Down syndrome, and Prader-Willi syndrome. *Research in Developmental Disabilities, 27*, 151–161.

DeVincent, C. J., Gadow, K. D., Delosh, D., & Geller, L. (2007). Sleep disturbance and its relation to *DSM-IV* psychiatric symptoms in preschool-age children with pervasive developmental disorder and community controls. *Journal of Child Neurology, 22*, 161–169.

Didden, R., Korzilius, H., van Aperlo, B., van Overloop, C., & de Vries, M. (2002). Sleep problems and daytime problem behaviours in children with intellectual disability. *Journal of Intellectual Research, 46*, 537–547.

Elia, M., Ferri, R., Musumeci, S. A., Del Gracco, S., Bottitta, M., Scuderi, C., . . . Grubar, J. C. (2000). Sleep in subjects with autistic disorder: A neurophysiological and psychological study. *Brain & Development, 22*, 88–92.

Filipek, P. A., Accardo, P. J., Ashwal, S., Baranek, G. T., Cook, E. H., Jr., Dawson, G . . . Volkmar, F. R. (2000). Practice parameters: Screening and diagnosis of autism. *American Academy of Neurology, 55*, 468–479.

Gilliam, J. E. (1995). *Gilliam Autism Rating Scale.* Austin, TX: Pro-Ed.

Gilliam, J. E. (2006). *Gilliam Autism Rating Scale–Second edition.* Austin, TX: Pro-Ed.

Goodlin-Jones, B., Schwichtenberg, A. J., Iosif, A. M., Tang, K., Liu, J., & Anders, T. F. (2009). Six-month persistence of sleep problems in young children with autism, developmental delay, and typical development. *Journal of the American Academy of Child & Adolescent Psychiatry, 48*, 847–854.

Gottlieb, D. J., Vezina, R. M., & Chase, C. (2003). Symptoms of sleep-disordered breathing in 5-year-old children with sleepiness and problem behaviors. *Pediatrics, 112*, 870–877.

Guénolé, F., Godbout, R., Nicolas, A., Franco, P., Claustrat, B., & Baleyte, J. (2011). Melatonin for disordered sleep in individuals with autism spectrum disorders: Systematic review and discussion. *Sleep Medicine Reviews, 15*, 379–387.

Hoban, T. F. (2000). Sleeplessness in children with neurodevelopmental disorders: Epidemiology and management. *CNS Drugs, 14*, 11–22.

Hoffman, C. D., Sweeney, D. P., Gilliam, J. E., Apodaca, D. D., Lopez-Wagner, M. C., & Castillo, M. M. (2005). Sleep problems and symptomology in children with autism. *Focus on Autism and Other Developmental Disabilities, 20*, 194–200.

Hoffman, C. D., Sweeney, D. P., Gilliam, J. E., & Lopez-Wagner, M. C. (2006). Sleep problems in children with autism and in typically developing children. *Focus on Autism and Other Developmental Disabilities, 21*, 146–152.

Hoffman, C. D., Sweeney, D. P., Lopez-Wagner, M. C., Hodge, D., Nam, C., & Botts, B. (2008). Children with autism: Sleep problems and mothers' stress. *Focus on Autism and Other Developmental Disabilities, 23*, 155–165.

Honomichl, R. D., Goodlin-Jones, B. L., Burnham, M. M., Gaylor, E., & Anders, T. F. (2002). Sleep patterns of children with pervasive developmental disorders. *Journal of Autism and Other Developmental Disorders, 29*, 143–147.

Kheirandish, L., & Gozal, D. (2006). Neurocognitive dysfunction in children with sleep disorders. *Developmental Science, 9*, 388–399.

Krakowiak, P., Goodlin-Jones, B., Hertz-Picciotto, I., Croen, L. A., & Hansen, R. L. (2008). Sleep problems in children with autism spectrum disorders, developmental delays, and typical development: A population based study. *Journal of Sleep Research, 17*, 197–206.

Lecavalier, L. (2005). An evaluation of the Gilliam Autism Rating Scale. *Journal of Autism and Developmental Disorders, 35*, 795–805.

Liu, X., Hubbard, J. A., Fabes, R. A., & Adam, J. A. (2006). Sleep disturbances and correlates of children with autism spectrum disorders. *Child Psychiatry & Human Development, 37*, 179–191.

Maganti, R., Hausman, N., Koehn, M., Sandok, E., Glurich, I., & Mukesh, B. N. (2006). Excessive daytime sleepiness and sleep complaints among children with epilepsy. *Epilepsy & Behavior, 8*, 272–277.

Malow, B. A., Marzec, M. L., McGrew, S. G., Wang, L., Hendersen, L. M., & Stone, W. L. (2006). Characterizing sleep in children with autism spectrum disorders: A multidimensional approach. *Sleep, 29*, 1563–1571.

Matson, J. L., & Nebel-Schwalm, M. S. (2005). Comorbid psychopathology with autism spectrum disorder in children: An overview. *Research in Developmental Disabilities, 28*, 341–352.

Mindell, J. A. (1993). Sleep disorders in children. *Health Psychology, 12*, 151–162.

National Institutes of Health. (2003). *National sleep disorders research plan.* Washington, DC: U.S. Department of Health and Human Services, National Center on Sleep Disorders Research.

National Research Council. (2001). *Educating children with autism.* Washington, DC: National Academic Press.

O'Connor, A. B., & Healy, O. (2010). Long-term post-intensive behavioral intervention outcomes for five children with autism spectrum disorder. *Research in Autism Spectrum Disorders, 4*, 594–604.

Owens, J. A., Spirito, A., & McGuinn, M. (2000). The Children's Sleep Habits Questionnaire (CSHQ): Psychometric properties of a survey instrument for school-aged children. *Sleep, 23*, 1043–1051.

Oyane, N. M. F., & Bjorvatn, B. (2005). Sleep disturbances in adolescents and young adults with autism and Asperger syndrome. *Autism: The International Journal of Research and Practice, 9*, 83–94.

Paavonen, E. J., Vehkalahti, K., Vanhala, R., von Wendt, L., Nieminen-von Wendt, T., & Aronen, E. T. (2008). Sleep problems in children with Asperger syndrome. *Journal of Autism and Developmental Disorders, 38*, 41–51.

Patzold, L. M., Richdale, A. L., & Tonge, B. J. (1998). An investigation into sleep characteristics of children with autism and Asperger's disorder. *Journal of Paediatric Child Health, 34*, 528–533.

Randazzo, A. C., Meuhlbach, M. J., Schweitzer, P. K., & Walsh, J. K. (1998). Cognitive function following acute sleep restriction in children ages 10-14. *Sleep, 21*, 861–868.

Richdale, A. L. (1999). Sleep problems in autism: Prevalence, cause and intervention. *Developmental Medicine & Child Neurology, 41*, 60–66.

Richdale, A. L., Francis, A., Gavidia-Payne, S., & Cotton, S. (2000). Stress, behaviour and sleep problems in children with an intellectual disability. *Journal of Intellectual & Developmental Disability, 25*, 147–161.

Richdale, A. L., & Schreck, K. A. (2009). Sleep problems in autism spectrum disorders: Prevalence, nature, & possible biopsychosocial aetiologies. *Sleep Medicine Reviews, 13*, 403–411.

Ritvo, E. R., & Freeman, B. J. (1978). National Society for Autistic Children definition of the syndrome of autism. *Journal of Autism and Childhood Schizophrenia, 8*, 162–167.

Sadeh, A., Gruber, R., & Raviv, A. (2002). Sleep, neurobehavioral functioning, and behavior problems in school-age children. *Child Development, 73,* 405–417.

Schreck, K. A., & Mulick, J. A. (2000). Parental report of sleep problems in children with autism. *Journal of Autism and Developmental Disorders, 30,* 127–135.

Schreck, K. A., Mulick, J. A., & Smith, A. F. (2004). Sleep problems as possible predictors of intensified symptoms of autism. *Research in Developmental Disabilities, 25,* 57–66.

Schwichtenberg, A. J., Iosif, A. M., Goodlin-Jones, B., Tang, K., & Anders, T. (2011). Daytime sleep patterns in preschool children with autism, developmental delay, and typical development. *American Journal of Intellectual and Developmental Disabilities, 116,* 142–152.

South, M., Williams, B. J., McMahon, W. M., Owley, T., Filipek, P. A., Shernoff, E., . . . Ozonoff, S. (2002). Utility of the Gilliam Autism Rating Scale in research and clinical populations. *Journal of Autism and Developmental Disorders, 32,* 593–599.

Statistical Package for the Social Sciences. (2006). Statistical Package for the Social Sciences (Release 15.0) [Computer software]. Chicago: Author.

Stuart, M., & McGrew, J. H. (2009). Caregiver burden after receiving a diagnosis of an autism spectrum disorder. *Research in Autism Spectrum Disorders, 3,* 86–97.

Waterhouse, L., Morris, R., Allen, D., Dunn, M., Fein, D., Feinstein, C., . . . Wing, L. (1996). Diagnosis and classification in autism. *Journal of Autism and Developmental Disorders, 26,* 59–86.

Wiggs, L. D. (2003). Pediatric sleep disorders: The need for multidisciplinary sleep clinics. *International Journal of Pediatric Otorhinolaryngology, 67,* 115–120.

Wiggs, L., & Stores, G. (2004). Sleep patterns and sleep disorders in children with autistic spectrum disorders: Insights using parent report and actigraphy. *Developmental Medicine & Child Neurology, 46,* 372–380.

Williams, P. G., Sears, L. L., & Allard, A. (2004). Sleep problems in children with autism. *Journal of Sleep Research, 13,* 265–268.

Acknowledgments

We offer much appreciation for the contributions of our guest reviewers for Volume 27.

Carina M. De Fazio
Georgia State University

Kristen DuMoulin
CUNY Center for Worker Education

Roberto Gama
Georgia State University

Jackie Isbell
Georgia State University

Helen McCabe
Hobart and William Smith Colleges

Rebecca McCathren
University of Missouri

Karen O'Conner
University of Missouri

Brooks Peters
Georgia State University

Amanda Richdale
La Trobe University, Australia

Tia Schultz
University of Missouri

Ginny Van Rie
Georgia College and State University

Jane Wegner
University of Kansas

Ernest Whitmarsh
Cobb County School District